W9-AMU-483

Presented to:

Andre

From:

Kathleen

Date:

September 2006

Make Your Day Count Devotional

for Teens

Presented by

Lindsay Roberts and Friends

Harrison House
Tulsa, Oklahoma

Make Your Day Count Devotional for Teens
ISBN 1-57794-661-8

Oral Roberts Ministries
Tulsa, Oklahoma 74171-0001

Published by Harrison House, Inc.
P.O. Box 35035
Tulsa, Oklahoma 74153

Manuscript compiled and edited by Betsy Williams of Williams Services, Inc., Tulsa, Oklahoma; www.williams.services.inc@cox.net.

Contents

Introduction

No doubt you live a very active life with many pressures and responsibilities. Not only are you responsible for your studies and schoolwork, most likely you already have a job. Any extracurricular activities like clubs, band, or sports, plus music or tennis lessons only add more responsibility, although the rewards are worth the effort. Whether you are a teen still living at home or have already headed off to college, your days are jam-packed. But do you always get off to a good start each morning? Good question!

What we do first thing in the morning sets the tone for the rest of the day. The purpose of this book is to give you a bite-sized bit of godly wisdom shared by some of the most awesome Christian leaders in the body of Christ today. Then we've included an action step, something practical you can do each day to apply what you've learned.

Sprinkled throughout you will find some helpful tips and quick-and-easy recipes that you and your friends are sure to enjoy. My goal, and that of the other contributors, is to help you start each day on the right track and *make your day count!*

Blessings,
Lindsay

The Power of God's Love

Lindsay Roberts

Everyone who loves has been born of God and knows God. Whoever does not love does not know God, because God is love.

—1 John 4:7,8

God *is* love, and everyone who knows Him knows love. That means the words *God* and *love* are one and the same. Once I heard Kenneth Copeland say that every time you see the word *God* in Scripture, you can replace it with the word *love* and vice versa.

Take 1 John 4:18, for example, which says, "Perfect love drives out fear." You could exchange the word *love* for *God,* and then it would say, "God drives out fear."

If God is the highest power of all powers and it takes His love to get rid of fear, think about how powerful fear can be. Then it's easy to see how it keeps people in bondage. But the love of God is more powerful than anything. It can calm any situation and bring peace and hope instead.

Some people think that love is all about hearts and flowers. But getting through the tough situations in life takes more than a box of candy and a greeting card! God's love is powerful! When you understand the power of love and ask God to pour it out through you to those around you, you can become a bridge over troubled waters. Regardless of what you face today, I encourage you to pull out your secret weapon of love.[1]

make **your** day count

Are there areas of your life where fear is present? God wants to set you free. Receive His love today. As His love fills you up, it will flush away all fear. Next, let His love flow through you to others.

Extreme Lengths

Terri Copeland Pearsons

Jesus said, "I lay down my life for the sheep."

—John 10:15

Jesus went to extreme lengths to prove God's love to even the most sinful men. Luke 8 tells of a time when He had ministered all day, then got into a boat to go over to the other side. It wasn't an easy trip. They encountered hurricane force winds until Jesus rebuked the storm, putting a stop to it.

When they arrived, a man met them who was so full of evil spirits that he could not be bound—a man who lived in the tombs, thriving off of bodies and carcasses, cutting and beating himself. He ran toward Jesus, probably intending to kill Him, but when he ran into the presence of God, those demonic powers fell in subjection. Jesus drove out the demons and set the man free.

Think about the extremes Jesus went to. Why did He travel across the lake when He was so tired that He fell asleep shortly after setting sail? Why did He go through the storm? I'm convinced it's because God heard the cry of one desperate man and said to Jesus, "I don't care how bound up by perversion he is or what he looks or smells like. I love him. Go and set him free."

God hears your cry too, and He has gone to great extremes to purchase your freedom. Be set free today![2]

make **your** day count

Think about the extremes that Jesus went to in order to set you free. By faith, give God those things that have bound you. In their place, take hold of the resurrection power that brought Jesus back to life and causes you to triumph over sin.

"Flame-Thrower" Friends

Eastman Curtis

The righteous should choose his friends carefully,
For the way of the wicked leads them astray.

—Proverbs 12:26 NKJV

It can be difficult to be a Christian in a non-Christian world. I think that is why the disciples really loved to spend time with each other. They were a great encouragement to one another. I believe one of the key elements to staying on fire for God is to hang around others who are on fire. We all need to have friends who can encourage us and pray with us every day.

The Bible instructs us to choose our friends carefully because the way of the wicked will lead us astray. Now, every one of us has a desire to feel accepted by our peers. And that isn't necessarily a bad thing, especially if we are hanging around "flame-throwers for Jesus." It can, however, be a bad thing if we are hanging around a bunch of "spiritual dead-heads and lukewarmies" because even strong Christians can be influenced negatively by wrong friends.

That is why the Word says that you are to choose your friends carefully. So think about the friends you currently have. Do you know where they stand in their relationship with God? Are your friends who aren't serving God snuffing out your flame? If so, you may need to reevaluate how much time you spend with them. It's much more important that you spend time with your "flame-thrower" friends who love Jesus.[3]

make **your** day count

Make a list of your closest friends. Are they on fire for God, or are their relationships with God cold or nonexistent? Do they encourage your growth in Christ, or do they pull you toward worldly things? Seek out a "flame-thrower" friend today. If you don't have one, ask God and He will bring one into your life.

time **saving** tips

Making New Friends

Betsy Williams

It's difficult when you're the "new kid on the block." Maybe you've moved from a different city or state. Maybe you've just moved across town but now go to a new school. Or maybe you'd just like to branch out and make new friends. Whatever your reason, here are some tips to help you get started.

Smile. When someone smiles at you, doesn't it make you want to smile back? Without saying a word, a smile makes others feel good, and people want to be around others who make them feel good.

Pay genuine compliments. Don't you feel good when someone says they like something about you?

Take a genuine interest in others. Ask people questions about themselves and really listen. Ask open-ended questions instead of ones with yes/no answers. You could ask a person about his or her hobbies or where an individual got such a cool-looking jacket, for example.

Remember people's names and use them whenever you see them. People like the sound of their own name and it conveys that you care enough to remember.

Making new friends isn't always easy, and sometimes it's downright scary. But if you'll make the effort, you'll be pleased with the results. Who knows, maybe you'll make a friend who will be a true friend for life.

easy **recipes**

Eastman's Ice Cream Sundaes[4]

Eastman Curtis

1 small container vanilla ice cream
1 small container chocolate ice cream
1 small container strawberry ice cream
1 jar strawberry topping
1 can crushed pineapple, drained
1 jar maraschino cherries
1 bag candy of your choice
1 container sprinkles
1 cup nuts, chopped
1 can whipped cream

Place scoops of the different ice creams on the bottom of each bowl.

Add different toppings for the sundaes as desired.

Place nuts over the toppings.

Add whipped cream and top with a cherry.

Protection in Dangerous Times

Kellie Copeland Kutz

The Lord gives wisdom, and from his mouth come knowledge and understanding. He holds victory in store for the upright, he is a shield to those whose walk is blameless, for he guards the course of the just and protects the way of his faithful ones.

—Proverbs 2:6–8

With all of the turmoil in the world, school violence, and the threat of terrorism, no doubt you are aware of the need for God's supernatural protection. Or maybe you feel invincible like many young people. Either way, the truth remains that we live in a dangerous world. What can you do to ensure that you and those you love are protected?

I began seeking the Lord about this after my cousin Nikki was killed in a car accident involving a drunk driver. Nikki was Miss "On Fire for God," one of the most phenomenal people I have ever known. Her death was a huge wake-up call for me, and I asked the Lord to show me how we let it happen, and what we needed to do to make sure it never happened again.

God taught me four primary things we must do to ensure our protection and that of those we love: plead the blood of Jesus; take advantage of angelic protection; listen to our spirits; and, for you as a teen, to honor and obey your parents. Developing rock-solid confidence in these principles is the goal you should be aiming for as a believer; and as you do, your faith will grow and you can know that you and those you love are safe.[5]

make **your** day count

Plead the blood of Jesus over yourself, your friends, and your family. Then send forth the angels for protection. Ask God to teach you to hear His voice, to make you aware of danger. Be mindful that the Word promises you long life if you will honor and obey your parents. (Eph. 6:1–3.)

There Is Freedom in Christ

Nancy Alcorn

The Spirit of the Sovereign Lord is on me.... He has sent me to bind up the brokenhearted, to proclaim freedom for the captives and release from darkness for the prisoners.
—Isaiah 61:1

Eating disorders, suicide, addictions, unplanned pregnancies. There is an epidemic of social problems that young adults face today. However, these are more than just problems. They are symptoms of a deeper crisis. Tragically, many young women and men are deeply wounded by incest, rape, physical and sexual child abuse, and other tragic experiences.

In order for them to be free, the root causes and not just the symptoms must be dealt with. The main thing to realize is that without a changed heart, there is no such thing as a changed life. Jesus Christ is the only One who can heal a broken heart and bring true freedom.

Young adults who are dealing with these intense issues need to know that they can be forgiven and receive new life in Christ. And God doesn't just forgive. He is able to provide a way for the shame, guilt, and fear to be removed. A person's past does not have to destroy their future.

There is no quick fix, however. It is going *through* the painful issues and not around them that produces lasting change. This is where the assistance of a professional Christian counselor can help.

There is hope. Healing is available. You can come out on the other side fully restored. Freedom can be an experienced reality.[7]

make **your** day count

Are you facing a critical issue you need to work through? No situation is too difficult or hopeless for God. Speak to a parent, youth leader, pastor, or trusted teacher if necessary, so healing can begin.

Just Say Yes!

Lindsay Roberts

No matter how many promises God has made, they are "Yes" in Christ.

—2 Corinthians 1:20

When I was eighteen, I was told that I would never have children. Today I have three daughters—all miracles—but they did not come easily. Before I received my miracles, I had miscarriages, a tumor, surgeries, and the death of a baby son.

I finally had to come to a place that instead of saying, "God heals people," I had to say, "God heals *me.*" It was when I made a decision to believe in healing for myself that the miracles began.

In John 5:1–15, Jesus approached a man who had been waiting thirty-eight years by the Pool of Bethesda for an angel to stir the water so he could be healed. In thirty-eight years, the man had not figured out how to be the first into the pool to be healed! He was just waiting and wondering.

Jesus asked him, "Do you want to get well?" (v. 6). Instead of saying yes, the man replied, "I have no one to help me into the pool" (v. 7). Jesus looked for people who would answer, "Yes! I believe!"

Today, even as a teenager, you have the same opportunity. Instead of saying, "I don't have anyone to help me," or, "God heals people but He hasn't healed me," instead say, "Yes! I believe and I receive my miracle." Then stay expectant in faith until it comes.[8]

make **your** day count

Whatever miracle you need today, know that God wants to perform it. Say, "Yes! I believe Your promise concerning my need. Yes, You are talking to me!"

time **saving** tips

Beauty Tips[9]

Dee Simmons

"You have to get your beauty sleep." Did you know that's the truth? When you've had eights hours of sleep, you really do look better.

I believe good nutrition and drinking enough water are also important in helping to have healthy-looking skin. Here is a simple formula that I use to determine the amount of water I need to drink: I divide my weight in half and drink that amount of water in ounces each day. For instance, 120 pounds divided by 2 equals 60 ounces of water a day.

Caterpillar Fun Snack

Cleo Justus

These are fun to make and fun to eat.

Take a handful of small Ritz crackers.

Spread cream cheese or peanut butter between them, adding on to make a long caterpillar.

Spread cream cheese or peanut butter on front and add two raisins for eyes.

Virginity: Its Own Defense Mechanism

Carla Stephens

An unmarried woman or virgin is concerned about the Lord's affairs: Her aim is to be devoted to the Lord in both body and spirit.

—1 Corinthians 7:34

Here Paul states that a virgin is able to concentrate more on the things of God than on the distractions and temporary pleasures of the world. A virgin can focus his or her attention on pleasing God, whereas a non-virgin must contend with the distraction of wanting to please a partner in bed.

This distraction is the natural result of awakening sexual desire. Think about it. If you'd never tasted chocolate ice cream, you would never crave it. The same is true with sex. It's much more difficult to resist the urge to have sex once you've experienced it.

Therefore, virginity is its own defense mechanism. It is designed to help you combat the strong forces of sexual temptation and prevent you from having to reap the consequences associated with sex outside of marriage.

Virginity is God's precious gift to us to be protected at all costs. When you hold on to this gift, it signifies that you have been set apart, consecrated—for God and the person He's created for you to marry. It means you have given thought to the future, weighed all your options, and chosen to set yourself apart unto God.

Your virginity is one of the most precious gifts you can give your future spouse. Save it for him or her. You'll be glad you did.[10]

make **your** day count

Find a friend who shares your commitment to virginity, and be an encouragement and strength to one another. If you have already given your virginity away, you can start anew. Ask for God's forgiveness and be restored to a place of purity.

An Open Door for Miracles

Gloria Copeland

We have gained access by faith into this grace in which we now stand.

—Romans 5:2

When people came to Jesus and asked, "What must we do to do the works God requires?" Jesus answered, "The work of God is this: to believe in the one he has sent" (John 6:28,29). All through the Bible, every time something awesome happened, somebody had to trust God enough to act on what He said and open the door.

That's what happened to me the day I made Jesus my Lord. I read Matthew 6:26 and found out that God cares even for birds—and faith burst into my heart. I didn't know the first thing about becoming a Christian. Yet when I spoke that faith out—that I believed in Him—I opened the door just a crack and God's mercy and love flooded my heart and changed me forever.

It's still true today. However wide you open that door of faith is how much of God's mercy and goodness will flow into your life. He wants to do great things in your life and give you all the benefits of salvation. When I say salvation, I'm not just talking about a ticket to heaven. Salvation means freedom—from depression, poverty, sickness, danger, fear—anything you need freedom from!

Psalm 68:19 says God loads us with the benefits of salvation daily. Start each day by opening the door of faith. Don't just open it a crack—rip it off the hinges![11]

make **your** day count

Spend some time reading your Bible until a verse seems to "leap off the page." That is the Holy Spirit making God's Word alive to you. As you believe that verse and act as if it is true—because it is—it will open the door wide to God's blessings.

My Friend Is a Homosexual

Eastman Curtis

Do you not know that the wicked will not inherit the kingdom of God? Do not be deceived: Neither the sexually immoral…nor homosexual offenders… And that is what some of you were. But you were washed, you were sanctified, you were justified in the name of the Lord Jesus Christ and by the Spirit of our God.

—1 Corinthians 6:9,11

Nowadays society has taken a "to-each-his-own" stance regarding homosexuality in an effort not to offend anyone. Homosexuality is becoming widely accepted and is even being taught as a "lifestyle option." Some curriculum is even introducing it into the classroom, encouraging students to explore it!

But God never calls this lifestyle an option. He calls it sin. So how do you deal with the fact that one or more of your friends at school may be professing homosexuals?

First of all, if you are ever going to be able to help those friends, you must have a voice in their lives. This means they need to respect your influence. But that will never happen if you join others in harassing them.

Just like you, these friends need God's love. Remember, however, that they are bound by a strong deception, and their only hope for freedom is through Jesus.

Also, here's a very important point to remember: Because homosexuality is such a strong deception, be sure to keep yourself accountable to your Christian friends when you do reach out to any teens who claim to be homosexual. There is always the possibility that they may try to pull you in.

Finally, understand that you don't have to love these people's sin, but God has called you to love them. You can make a difference in their lives.[12]

make **your** day count

If you have a homosexual friend, begin praying for God to begin working in his or her life. Philippians 2:13 is a good promise to claim on behalf of your friend. Bind deception according to Matthew 18:18, then ask God to give you opportunities to speak into this individual's life.

time **saving** tips

Baby-sitting Basics[13]

Baby-sitting is a great way for teens to make money and learn about children. It is also a great responsibility that should be taken seriously.

Know the person you'll be working for before taking the job. Check references if this will be your first time working for this person. Make sure your parents know about and are in agreement with you taking the job.

Get specific instructions about the number and ages of the children, bedtimes, food, medicines, allergies, and other information. Ask questions. Parents feel more confident with sitters who are concerned about the care of their children.

Arrive early to confirm all of this information and get any additional instructions.

Make sure your parents know how to contact you.

Know where the parents are going, when they will return, and how to contact them in the event of an emergency.

Get contact information about a neighbor or other adult who may be contacted if the parents can't be reached.

Keep all of this information by the telephone.

Knowing first-aid procedures will help prepare you for emergencies. The Red Cross offers baby-sitting certification, which is highly recommended.[14]

easy **recipes**

Mama's Vanilla Drop Cookies

Cleo Justus

1 cup sour cream
1 cup sugar
1 tsp. soda
1 egg
2½ cups flour
1 tsp. vanilla

Beat eggs in mixing bowl. Add sour cream and sugar.

Mix in dry ingredients. Add vanilla.

Drop on cookie sheet, giving plenty of room to spread.

Bake in 350° oven 8 to 10 minutes, or to desired doneness.

Leave on cookie sheet for a few minutes and remove to serving dish or cookie jar, if there are any left.

This may be mixed up ahead and stored in the refrigerator and baked as needed.

If batter is cold, make balls the size of walnuts and mash on cookie sheet and bake.

Chopped fruits and nuts may be added.

God Really Does Love You!

Terri Copeland Pearsons

I pray that you...may...grasp how wide and long and high and deep is the love of Christ.

—Ephesians 3:17,18

"God is love" (1 John 4:8). But be honest. Is God really *love* to you?

Most people think God is following them around with a big stick, ready to smack them every time they sin. Yet when you look at the life of Jesus, He went to extreme lengths to prove to us the love of God. Ultimately He even went to hell for us.

God loves you with an amazing love! He didn't have you born again just so He could get you off His conscience. Religion has taught people that God saves us just so we can praise Him and live for Him forever. In other words, to satisfy His own egotistical, selfish need to have people tell Him how great He is all the time.

No! God isn't like that! Ephesians tells us that He redeemed us in order to restore our fellowship with Him—both now and throughout the ages. His heart cries out to those who are in bondage to or have been hurt by sin. He knows how wonderful He can cause their lives to be. His driving compassion moves Him to be with us and to bless us.

If you haven't *really* experienced this love in a personal way, ask God to reveal the full scope of His marvelous love for you. He will...because He loves you.[15]

make **your** day count

Today, meditate on the truth that God is love. Ask Him to reveal the unique and personal ways that He demonstrates His great love for you. Be sure to write them down in a journal for later reflection.

Six Reasons To Break Up with Someone

Blaine Bartel

Can two walk together, unless they are agreed?

—Amos 3:3 NKJV

I discourage you from "going out" or "dating" too early. The Bible has much to say about developing good friendships, but nothing about dating. As you grow older and a good friendship develops into a romantic relationship, be careful to keep things on the right track.

In case you're not sure, here are six reasons to break off a relationship that has gotten off track.

1. If you are being pressured in any way to take the relationship to a "physical" level that you know is inappropriate.
2. If you are verbally, mentally, or physically abused in any way, get out of the relationship—and quickly.
3. If your partner doesn't show the spiritual drive and Christian attributes that you know are necessary to be strong for Christ, it's time to let go.

4. If you feel used in any way for what you have, give, own, or provide, don't stay in the relationship. Be sure the person likes (or loves) *you.* Period.

5. If you find the person to be a liar, don't stick around. Trust can only be built on truth.

6. If the person breaks up with you, let go. Seriously. There are many fish in the sea, and you may have just gotten rid of "Jaws," so move on![16]

make **your** day count

Do any of these six things apply to you? If so, take the matter to God in prayer. He loves you and wants the best for you. It may feel like a leap of faith to break up with someone you care for deeply, but God will not let you down. He's the God of the universe. He will bring the right person at the right time.

The Spirit of Jezebel Unmasked

Lindsay Roberts

These things have I written unto you concerning them that seduce you.

—1 John 2:26 KJV

The spirit of Jezebel is not a person, but a spirit. The first time this spirit manifested in the Bible was through a woman, Queen Jezebel. (1 Kings 16-19.) This spirit is real and it has an agenda to seduce you from your relationship with God and what He has called you to do. It can use your friends, popularity, money, power. It can even be seen in the form of religion by distorting your view of God, making you think you have to jump through hoops to win His approval, eventually tearing you away from God.

Let me tell you about the five things the spirit of Jezebel uses to try to destroy you.

1. Fear. A spirit that comes to torment, control, and paralyze you.
2. Discouragement. When you should be rejoicing, you wish you'd never been born. (1 Kings 19:4.)
3. Confusion. You don't know what to do. Your head is spinning.
4. Self-Doubt. You doubt your self-worth, causing you to retreat, which opens the door for terror.
5. Terror.

If any of these things is controlling you, ask God to help you. Ask Him to forgive you for anything you have done that goes against His ways. This leads to restoration. And there is good news: Everything Jesus did on the cross was to restore you.[17]

make **your** day count

Is there anything in your life trying to seduce you and lead in a direction other than God's? Receive God's strength today, then turn from that thing and run toward Him. You will be safe with Him, and He will set you free.

My Story

Nancy Alcorn

There is a way that seems right to a man,
but in the end it leads to death.

—Proverbs 14:12

Shortly after becoming a Christian and graduating from college, I innocently fell into the struggle of my life.

One evening a couple invited me over for dinner. Afterward I volunteered to clean their house while they attended a meeting. I began to feel nauseated from overeating, but I also had a strong desire to please my friends. No matter how nauseated I was, I kept trying to clean. Finally, I decided that my only hope of fulfilling my commitment was to make myself throw up, thus eliminating the nausea.

After I had "helped myself," it hit me that I could do that all the time, eat anything I wanted, and still control my weight. I began purging several times a week, which led to many physical problems. Even worse were the all-consuming thoughts about food and the overwhelming fear of gaining weight.

It was a five-year period of hell so bad that at times I wished I had been dead. But somehow, I knew there was hope in God. There was, but it was only through dealing with the root causes. Because I stayed in the Word, renewed my mind to the truth, and cried out to God continuously, I was eventually set free. Thankfully there is more help for eating disorders today. It isn't easy, but through Christ, you can be set free.[18]

make **your** day count

Are you or is someone you know dealing with an eating disorder?
Don't try to overcome this or any addiction on your own.
Seek support from your parents, a pastor, a teacher, or godly counselor.

time **saving** tips

Baby-sitting Do's and Don'ts

Betsy Williams

DO make sure all doors and windows are locked and outside lights are on.

DO have a list of emergency phone numbers including the children's physician, the hospital your employer uses, and Poison Control; and keep it by the phone.

DO get written permission from the parents to call an ambulance and have the child taken to the hospital in the event of a life-threatening emergency and they cannot be reached.

DO interact with the children. Read, play games, or do crafts with them.

DO more than is expected. Leave the house in better shape than when your employer left. Clean the kitchen counters, wash dirty dishes, empty the dishwasher, straighten up magazines, newspapers, etc. Put away anything that you or the children have gotten out.

DO NOT open the door to strangers or allow them into the house unless your employer specifically informs you to let them in.

DO NOT tell a caller that you are the baby-sitter and you are alone with the children. Let the answering machine answer the call.

DO NOT go outside to investigate suspicious noises or activities. Call the police.

DO NOT let a toddler or baby out of your sight—not even for a minute—to answer the telephone, talk to your friends, or for any other reason. Children have been known to drown by sticking their heads in a toilet or even in a pet's bowl of water.

easy **recipes**

Volcano Cupcakes

Cleo Justus

1 box chocolate cake mix
Paper cupcake holders
Large marshmallows
Chopped nuts

Prepare cake batter as directed on package.

Place 1 paper cupcake holder in each section of muffin pan.

Fill each paper cup ½ full of cake batter.

Add one marshmallow and push down to bottom of cup.

Add more batter to make paper cup ¾ full and sprinkle with chopped nuts.

Bake as directed on package.

These are very good, and each one will look different on top.

No need to add frosting, unless you just want to.

Transformed from the Inside Out

Kate McVeigh

Let God transform you into a new person by changing the way you think. Then you will know what God wants you to do, and you will know how good and pleasing and perfect his will really is.

—Romans 12:2 NLT

I was fifteen the day I opened my yearbook and read, "Voted least likely to succeed—Kate McVeigh." Tears flowed as I cried out, "God, if You don't do something, I'm going to kill myself."

From the fifth grade, I had been in classes for slow learners. The other kids made fun of me, calling me "Sped" because I was enrolled in Special Education. I developed an overwhelming inferiority complex and imagined myself a hopeless loser.

Then one day I attended one of Kenneth Hagin's meetings. His message offered something completely new to me—hope. I was saved and filled with the Holy Spirit, and immediately a great weight lifted off my shoulders. Depression and fear, which had been my constant companions, were gone. The thoughts of suicide—gone.

Soon I learned about claiming favor in every area of life. I began to see who God says I am in His Word and refused to think about myself in any other way. It wasn't long before people took notice.

My teachers were shocked by the improvement in my academic performance. I was even voted Most Valuable Player on the basketball team, whereas before, my hands quivered so much from fear that I was rarely allowed to play.

God's Word is *powerful.* It literally transformed me from the inside out. His Word will transform you too.[19]

make **your** day count

Read Psalm 5:12; Psalm 30:5; and Proverbs 3:1–4. Begin to claim God's promise of favor over every area of your life today, and begin to see yourself being transformed by His Word.

You Have Protection—In Him

Gloria Copeland

He alone is my refuge, my place of safety; he is my God, and I am trusting him. For he rescues you from every trap, and protects you from the fatal plague.

—Psalm 91:2,3 TLB

Is it possible to live free from fear in this dangerous and unpredictable world? Is it possible when gang members are in your school and metal detectors are in your halls? Is it possible when classmates are experimenting with Satanism, and drunk drivers are commonplace? Yes, it most definitely is! Because protection is a solid promise of God.

But it's not a promise that's offered to just anyone. It is promised to those who *abide* in the Lord. To *abide* is to live in continual union with Him, keeping His Word and obeying His voice. Those who abide in the Lord can live without dread of what Satan will do.

Let me make this clear though—God's promise of protection doesn't mean that Satan will leave you alone! It means that God will give you a way of escape every time Satan comes against you. (1 Cor. 10:13.)

If you're afraid of the dangers around you, spend more time in the Bible and in prayer until your trust in God overcomes your fear. Abide in the Lord and—no matter how dangerous this world becomes—He shall surely rescue you.[20]

make **your** day count

Read Psalm 91 in its entirety, using an Amplified Bible, if you have access to one. Maybe even make a copy of the psalm and have it laminated. It is a passage that you can apply to your life every single day. Fear is not from God. Meditate on His promises of protection and grow strong in courage today.

time **saving** tips

Five Good Habits That Will Make You a Winner[22]

Blaine Bartel

Preparation. "I will do all I must before, so that I can enjoy the results after."

Action. "I will do what I need to do right now because tomorrow may be too late."

Prayer. "I realize that my destiny is too great for me to attempt alone. God will be my constant help and source of strength to fulfill my dreams and achieve my destiny."

Character. "I will live life with honesty and integrity, the kind of attributes that will not just get me to the top, but keep me there."

Discipline. "I will continue to do what it takes to succeed, even when the excitement has dwindled, the new has worn off, and things become routine."

easy **recipes**

Chex Muddy Buddies

Abby Detcher

9 cups Chex cereal (any variety)
6 oz. semi-sweet chocolate chips
½ cup peanut butter
¼ cup margarine or butter
1 tsp. vanilla
1 ½ cups powdered sugar

Measure cereal into large bowl; set aside.

Microwave chocolate chips, peanut butter, and margarine in bowl uncovered on high 1 minute; stir.

Microwave 30 seconds longer or until mixture can be stirred smooth.

Sir in vanilla.

Pour chocolate mixture over cereal in bowl, stirring until evenly coated.

Pour into large plastic Ziploc bag; add powdered sugar.

Seal bag; shake until well coated.

Spread on waxed paper to cool.

Store in airtight container in refrigerator.

Fulfill Your Destiny

Eastman Curtis

Delight yourself in the Lord
and he will give you the desires of your heart.
—Psalm 37:4

You were created for a purpose. God has already thought out that purpose in detail. First of all, when God is your focus, He blesses you with the opportunity to see the desires of your heart come to pass. Secondly, and most people always forget this part, God Himself has placed natural gifts, talents, and interests in you for a reason.

For instance, why do you like music, football, or debate? Because God created and ignited those desires inside of you. He placed those desires in your heart to help fulfill His plan for your life.

So how do you know what God wants you to do with your life? Look at your greatest desires and interests. Are they the kind of desires that would be pleasing to God? If so, then He is the One Who placed those dreams in your heart. They are there for a reason; God expects you to act on the desires He has ignited within you and trust Him to bring them to pass in your life.

I don't care what you have been taught before—life isn't an accident. You aren't an accident. There are some things that God wants to accomplish here on earth in your lifetime that only you can do. You have a destiny, and He will equip you to fulfill it.[23]

make **your** day count

Write down the predominant desires you have and assess whether or not those things are pleasing to God. If they are, begin to build on those desires, involving God every step of the way. If you think your desires are not pleasing to God, ask Him to create in your heart a desire for His plan.

Take Advantage of Angelic Protection

Kellie Copeland Kutz

Bless the Lord, you His angels,
Who excel in strength, who do His word,
Heeding the voice of His word.

—Psalm 103:20 NKJV

If we are going to protect every area of our lives and the lives of those we love, we must understand and appropriate the angelic ministry. According to Hebrews 1:14, angels are servants sent to minister for us because we are heirs of salvation.

We may seem insignificant when we compare ourselves to angels, but God doesn't see it that way. Hebrews 2:5–6 explains that angels are not placed higher than us spiritually. He sent them to helpfully care for and look after us!

Because of this, God has given us the authority to command them to act on our behalf. Therefore, it is very important that you watch what comes out of your mouth. Make sure that your words reflect God's Word, because your angels were created to obey it.

So charge the angels to go forth on your behalf. Say, "I charge you, angels, in the name of Jesus, to watch over me and my loved ones today—to go before us, to protect us, and to keep us from all harm!" Then make sure you don't speak any negative words that would contradict what God has said in His Word. He wants to protect you and the ones you love.[24]

make **your** day count

Look up the verses mentioned above, and reflect on what they mean to you. Then charge the angels to go forth to keep you and your loved ones safe.

What If You've Already Messed Up?

Kate McVeigh

If we confess our sins to him, he can be depended on to forgive us and to cleanse us from every wrong. And it is perfectly proper for God to do this for us because Christ died to wash away our sins.

—1 John 1:9 TLB

Did you know that fornication (sex outside of marriage) is mentioned thirty-nine times in the New Testament? Obviously it is an important issue to God. And He has good reasons for telling you to wait, although I won't cover that now.

But maybe you've already fallen in this area and had sex outside of marriage. The good news is, there is forgiveness for you. The verse above states that all you have to do is ask the Lord to forgive you, and He will. Don't allow the devil to make you feel guilty about it once you've repented. Get back up again, and don't look back.

There were even some people in the Bible who messed up big time. In 2 Samuel 11, we can read about David and his affair with Bathsheba. And she got pregnant! Then, to top it off, he sent Bathsheba's husband, Uriah, into the heaviest fighting—basically a suicide mission—and Uriah was killed.

David committed adultery and murder! But he eventually came to his senses and remembered how much he loved God. He repented and God brought restoration to his life. After that, the Lord still referred to him as a man after His own heart. (Acts. 13:22.)

God will do the same for you, no matter how bad you've blown it. He can restore your life and get you back on track when you genuinely repent as David did.[25]

make **your** day count

If you have failed in the area of fornication or in any other area, take it to God in prayer right now. Don't put it off. No matter what you've done, God wants you to run to Him so He can restore you. Do it now and you can start again.

Don't Get Stressed Out; Stand Still!

Lindsay Roberts

Do not be afraid. Stand still, and see the salvation of the Lord, which He will accomplish for you today.

—Exodus 14:13 NKJV

Are you so overwhelmed by everything you need to do that you feel as though you might crack? I understand what it's like to be stressed. Whether you are a teen or an adult, it's difficult to find balance in your life with your hectic schedule and multitude of responsibilities.

Fear is a major cause of stress, yet there are many places in the Bible where God tells us to "fear not." When we "fear not," we are able to step outside the realm of being panic-stricken by circumstances. Then we are to "stand still."

Have you ever tried to make sense to a person who is running around all stressed out? In contrast, if you will stand still and get into an atmosphere of faith, you will "see the salvation of the Lord."

When I looked up this Scripture in the original text, I found that it means, "One who comes from outside to bring help." When you're in the middle of a stressful situation, the problems are often all you can see. Of course, if you were in the middle of a fire, the situation would look really bad to you. But, if you were *outside* the fire, you would be able to handle it more rationally. God deals with your circumstances from outside the stress, so step outside with Him. He has the solution you need![26]

make **your** day count

Make a conscious effort to "step out of" your circumstances today. Stand still with God outside those circumstances, and listen for what He says you need to do. Then watch as He saves the day.

time **saving** tips

Six Ways Any Person Can Become Cool[27]

Blaine Bartel

Let's get right to the point: You want to be accepted and popular with people. Who doesn't? Now, you know you can't try to gain popularity and "coolness" the way the world tries to manufacture it. So how does a person become "Christ-like cool"? Here are six ways:

You become cool when you stand up for what is right and don't care who stands with you.

You become cool when you reach out to the poor, the hurting, the lost—those who are "uncool."

You become cool when you take time for those whom many overlook—children. God loves kids, and so should we.

You become cool when you freely admit your short-comings, pick up where you've failed, and move forward with godly confidence.

You become cool when you put God first in your words, your actions, and your plans.

You become cool when you could care less about being cool.

easy **recipes**

Lindsay's Favorite Chicken Wings[28]

Lindsay Roberts

2 lbs. chicken wings
½ cup brown sugar
½ cup granulated sugar
½ cup soy sauce
1 cup chicken broth

Wash chicken, pat dry, and set aside.

In baking dish, mix all other ingredients and add chicken. Be sure all pieces are well coated and cover.

Refrigerate to marinate for at least 2 hours.*

Bake uncovered at 400° for 45 minutes. Serve warm or cold.

*I prefer overnight—it's not the same if you marinate less time.

God-Generated Boldness

Kenneth Copeland

Pray also for me, that whenever I open my mouth, words may be given me so that I will fearlessly make known the mystery of the gospel.

—Ephesians 6:19

If Christians today would get a true understanding of what happened when Jesus was raised from the dead, the same thing would happen to us that happened to the people in Acts 5. We'd get bold. Not with "faking-it" boldness that falls flat on its face, but with God-generated boldness that brings miracles on the scene.

If you want to see what can take place when that kind of boldness is around, read Acts 5. There were miracles and decisions to follow Jesus. The sick were healed and lives were changed.

For years I read this and thought only the apostles were involved in this great move of God, but all the Christians were filled with the Holy Spirit and spoke God's Word with boldness. This group preached about Jesus' rising all over town until thousands of people made Jesus their Lord. Then those people filled the streets, bringing in the sick to be healed!

You can have that kind of boldness. You get it by faith, just like the Christians in Acts 4 and 5. Want to turn your school upside down for God? Then get hold of God's Word. Dare to believe it. Then preach it in faith with boldness. Soon, people will be waiting at your locker, because they'll know that's where they can be saved, healed, and rescued.[29]

make **your** day count

Read Acts 4 and 5. Pray that God will give you that kind of boldness. Then step out and share God's love with someone today.

Does the Bible Say It's Wrong to Drink or Smoke Marijuana?

Eastman Curtis

Sin can't tell you how to live. After all, you're not living under that old tyranny any longer. You're living in the freedom of God.

—Romans 6:14 MESSAGE

The Bible as a whole tells a story about a God who wants His people to be set free from death and anything that causes death. Marijuana (or pot) and alcohol are two things the world offers us as a temporary escape, but God wants you to be free of everything that pollutes your spirit, soul, and body, including pot and alcohol. Once you realize that fact, it is easy to wise up to the deception and refuse to fall for it.

Don't compromise your freedom for a cheap escape. Compromise is like tooth decay. You don't feel it at first. But if you don't deal with the problem, the day will come when your whole mouth is rotted out. At that point, the slightest pressure applied to your teeth can make them begin to crumble.

That's what compromise does. If you fall into sin and don't repent of it, that sin can eventually cause everything good in your life to crumble.

Keep this in mind. When you spend time in an atmosphere of sin and compromise, you begin to get used to it. At first, it really hits you wrong, but after a while you become desensitized to what is going on, justifying the compromise in your mind. Eventually you will become trapped in that compromise. It's just not worth it.[30]

make **your** day count

Reevaluate your involvement in things that pollute your body and have the potential to destroy your life. Make the decision today to turn from those things if you're participating in them, and start walking toward a life of blessing in God.

Why Drugs Are Bad for You

Do not be wise in your own eyes;
fear the Lord and shun evil.
This will bring health to your body
and nourishment to your bones.
—Proverbs 3:7,8

Drugs are chemicals that change the way our bodies work. If you have taken medicine, you already know some kinds of drugs. But even those can be dangerous if not taken according to a doctor's instructions. Illegal drugs like ecstasy, marijuana, cocaine, LSD, and heroin are *always* dangerous.

- Even small amounts of drugs kill your brain cells, and they will never grow back.
- People on drugs can do really dumb or dangerous things that could hurt themselves or others.
- Schoolwork becomes even harder.
- Drugs can also prevent your body from growing properly and make you look sick all the time.
- Some drugs make kids angry, causing them to get into fights.
- Using drugs *even one time* can permanently damage your body—or kill you. *One* hit of crack or cocaine

can give even a kid a heart attack causing death. Sniff glue or any inhalant just once, and you could go blind—*permanently.*

- People on drugs may become addicted so that their bodies *need* the drug to function. Stopping drug use brings on withdrawal symptoms—throwing up, sweating, shaking, even hallucinating until the body gets used to being without the drug. Hallucinations are when a person thinks he or she hears or sees things that in reality aren't there.[31]

Stay away from drugs. The risks just aren't worth it.

make **your** day count

Every day is full of choices. Good choices lead you toward blessing; poor choices lead to a downward spiral. What one, good choice could you make today? Whatever it is, make that choice. It will get you one step closer to where you want to be.

time **saving** tips

What to Say When Someone Offers You Drugs or Alcohol[32]

"I like you, but I don't like drugs."

"I'd get kicked off the team if I were caught around drugs."

"No thanks. It's not for me."

"You're kidding, right? Why would I do something like that?"

"I can't. I have a big test tomorrow." Or, "I have a big game tomorrow."

"That's illegal. I don't want to get in trouble."

"I'm up for a scholarship and don't want to blow it."

"Can't do it. Gotta get home."

easy **recipes**

Pigs-in-a-Blanket

Betsy Williams

1 package of hot dogs
2 8-oz. packages of refrigerated crescent dinner rolls
Slices of cheddar cheese

Preheat oven to 375°.

With a knife, slit each hot dog lengthwise. Don't cut all the way through.

Place strips of cheddar cheese inside the slits.

Open cans of rolls and tear off triangles along perforations.

Place hot dogs lengthwise on the bottom of the triangles.

Roll up.

Bake 11–13 minutes or until cheese melts and rolls are browned.

Six Careers You Can Start in Your Teens

Blaine Bartel

Whatever your hand finds to do, do it with all your might.

—Ecclesiastes 9:10

While your youth is a time to have fun and enjoy life, it is also a time to learn the value of work and ambition. The Bible has much to say about the importance of working diligently.

Here are six careers that you can embark on right now.

1. Newspaper business. Throw a paper route, and discover the satisfaction of getting a job done early.
2. Investment broker. There are companies that will take investment capital of just $50. Learn how the market works, and start investing a little at a time.
3. Graphic arts. If you have an interest in drawing and art, begin offering your assistance to those in need. I know fourteen- and fifteen-year-olds who design logos and Web sites for companies and churches.
4. Film and video production. With an inexpensive camera and some software, you can be in the "movie" biz. My son began to be paid for his projects when he was still fifteen years old.

5. Lawn care. If you have a mower and a weed-eater, distribute flyers in your neighborhood and sign accounts to cut and trim grass after school and all summer.
6. Child care. Make yourself available to families for quality baby-sitting services. Be a good sitter, because they are hard to come by![33]

make **your** day count

Do any of these career opportunities peak your interest? Do any other jobs come to mind? Why not pick one and begin investigating the possibilities today. Make a phone call, look up information on the Internet, and ask questions of people you know.

Healing Power

Kenneth Copeland

He [Jesus] took up our infirmities
and carried our diseases.

—Matthew 8:17

It used to be as tough to get people to make decisions for Jesus as it is to get them healed today. Religious tradition had convinced people that salvation couldn't be obtained by the average person. Then, Dwight L. Moody started preaching that Jesus took their sins upon Himself, and if they'd simply receive the gift of salvation, He would be their Lord!

You'd hear that message in every church service. If you walked in the door and admitted you weren't a Christian, somebody would grab you and tell you that Jesus died for your sins! They would tell you to trust Him and He would change your life forever.

What do you think would happen if everyone picked up on the truth about healing in the same way? Healing would become as easily received as salvation!

If you're wishing such a move of God would begin, stop wishing and start your own! Dig into the Bible. Study and think about God's promises about healing. Listen to messages by men and women who understand healing. Then start sharing the healing power of God with others who need to hear it.

I'm not saying this will be easy. No, you'll have to stand strong for it in order to win. But when you stand strong in faith, you will see God's healing power touch through you![34]

make **your** day count

Look up Scriptures on healing like 1 Peter 2:24; 3 John 2; and Psalm 103:1–3. If you need healing in your body, receive it by faith, based on these verses. Then begin to thank God for healing you!

Are You Lonesome Tonight?

Kate McVeigh

May your unfailing love be my comfort,
according to your promise to your servant.

—Psalm 119:76

Maybe you've heard of Elvis Presley's song, "Are You Lonesome Tonight." But did you know that you can be alone without being lonely? I travel all the time and stay in hotels by myself, but I enjoy being alone and spending time with God. You can too. He is always there for you. When you draw near to Him, He will draw near to you. (James 4:8 NKJV.)

You are never really alone. The Holy Spirit lives right inside you and is with you wherever you go! In Matthew 28:20 NKJV Jesus says, "I am with you always, even to the end of the age." In Hebrews 13:5 He says, "Never will I leave you; never will I forsake you." Wherever you go, He is with you.

Maybe you don't have a boyfriend or girlfriend. Maybe you've just broken up with someone and you are lonely. Jesus promised in John 14:18 that He wouldn't leave you comfortless, and in verse 16, He says that He has asked God to give you another Comforter. You can lean on Him when you need comfort.

Going out with a friend of like precious faith can help too. If you don't have a friend like that, ask God to give you one and He will.

Being alone doesn't have to mean you are lonesome. God cares. Go to Him.[35]

make **your** day count

Spend a few moments in God's presence thinking about the verses above and let the Holy Spirit envelop you with His comfort. Then go out with a friend and have fun.

time **saving** tips

Laundry Basics

Betsy Williams

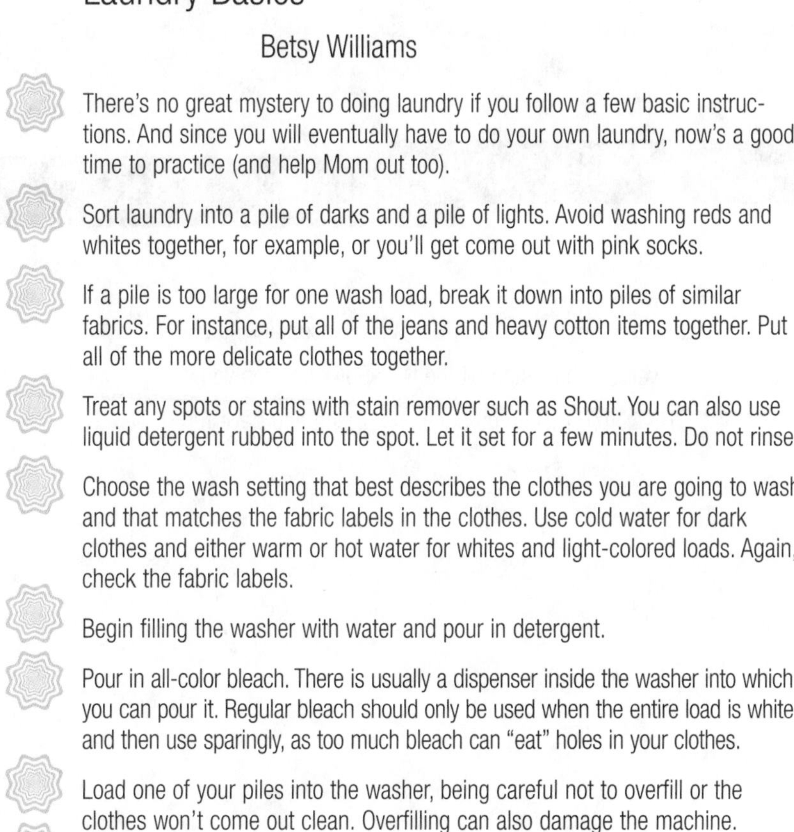

There's no great mystery to doing laundry if you follow a few basic instructions. And since you will eventually have to do your own laundry, now's a good time to practice (and help Mom out too).

Sort laundry into a pile of darks and a pile of lights. Avoid washing reds and whites together, for example, or you'll get come out with pink socks.

If a pile is too large for one wash load, break it down into piles of similar fabrics. For instance, put all of the jeans and heavy cotton items together. Put all of the more delicate clothes together.

Treat any spots or stains with stain remover such as Shout. You can also use liquid detergent rubbed into the spot. Let it set for a few minutes. Do not rinse.

Choose the wash setting that best describes the clothes you are going to wash and that matches the fabric labels in the clothes. Use cold water for dark clothes and either warm or hot water for whites and light-colored loads. Again, check the fabric labels.

Begin filling the washer with water and pour in detergent.

Pour in all-color bleach. There is usually a dispenser inside the washer into which you can pour it. Regular bleach should only be used when the entire load is white and then use sparingly, as too much bleach can "eat" holes in your clothes.

Load one of your piles into the washer, being careful not to overfill or the clothes won't come out clean. Overfilling can also damage the machine.

Fill the washer with enough water to cover your clothes.

As each load finishes washing, shake each article of clothing out before placing into the dryer. Clean out the lint trap before each load to protect from fire hazard. Toss in a fabric-softener sheet. Choose the setting for the dryer based on the fabric labels in the clothes.

Remove clothes from the dryer as soon as it stops to cut down on wrinkles.

easy **recipes**

Mexican Casserole[37]

Former Golden Eagles baseball coach Sunny Golloway and team members Dallas Martin, Lonnie Murphy, and Scott Campbell made this quick and simple recipe on the Make Your Day Count television broadcast.

2 cans chili with beans
1 large bag Fritos corn chips
1 can enchilada sauce (mild or hot)
1½ cups cheddar cheese, shredded

Preheat over to 350°.

In a 9- by 13-inch baking dish, mix the chili, the enchilada sauce, half the bag of corn chips, and 1 cup of cheese.

Top with the rest of the corn chips and cheddar cheese.

Bake at 350° until cheese is melted and casserole is hot.

A Root of Bitterness

Suzanne Rentz

Watch out that no bitterness takes root among you,
for as it springs up it causes deep trouble,
hurting many in their spiritual lives.

—Hebrews 12:15 TLB

Bitterness is like an ugly, creepy tick. You don't know when a tick latches onto you. It's often hidden in a spot that you don't see. It starts on the surface of your skin, then goes deeper. It grows as it sucks your blood. Soon it has a hold on you, and you can't remove it except by completely destroying it. Once you kill it, it must be removed before the wound will heal. Otherwise this tiny bug can cause an infection and a high fever in your whole body.

Unforgiveness is the disease that causes bitterness, and we don't always know it is in our heart. It starts out with a numb feeling, maybe an "I don't care" attitude. Maybe someone hurts us and instead of letting go, the hurt stays in our heart and grows. That's why we must be on guard.

Many Christians have talent, but some have never used it. Often God could have used them mightily, but they never dealt with the unforgiveness in their heart. Like a crippling disease, it has taken over their lives. They have missed God's best, and instead of making their lives count, those talents and gifts lie buried, wasted.

God wants to help you forgive so that any unforgiveness or bitterness can be uprooted and removed. Only then can you be truly free.[38]

make **your** day count

If there is any unforgiveness or bitterness in your heart, talk it over with God. He understands your pain and wants to heal you. Make a quality decision to forgive today, and leave the matter in God's hands. He will vindicate you.

He's Given You Peace

Kenneth Copeland

Jesus said, "Peace I leave with you; my peace
I give you. I do not give to you as the world gives.
Do not let your hearts be troubled and do not be afraid."
—John 14:27

Jesus had perfect faith, yet He had the toughest time of any man who has ever walked on earth. He was persecuted, criticized, and plotted against. He was tempted with every sin, yet He resisted it all.

There's nothing tougher than feeling the pressure of sin or sickness and then standing, refusing to let it take over, saying, "No! I won't receive this sickness in my body. I won't give in to this circumstance! I've been set free by the blood of Jesus, and I will live free by faith in Him!"

If you want to see just how much pressure such a stand of faith can bring, look at Jesus before He went to the cross. The pressure He faced put such a strain on His physical body that drops of blood poured through His skin like perspiration. Even then, sin could not conquer Him.

None of us will ever face that much pressure. Yet we have available to us the same power and peace that took Jesus not just through the pressure, but through the whipping, the mocking, and the Crucifixion. We have the peace that took Him all the way through!

He's given you His peace—far more than you'll ever need. So don't rehearse the problem over and over in your mind. Instead, receive His peace.[39]

make **your** day count

No matter what you are going through, God wants you to have the peace that passes understanding that Jesus purchased for you. Thank God that He is more than enough to supply your every need today, regardless of what it is.

Safe Sex Is Saved Sex

Eastman Curtis

It is God's will that you should be sanctified:
that you should avoid sexual immorality;
that each of you should learn to control his own
body in a way that is holy and honorable, not in
passionate lust like the heathen, who do not know God.
—1 Thessalonians 4:3-5

The Bible makes it very clear: Sex is an incredible gift from God reserved for the husband and wife in the covenant of marriage. God actually tells us to flee from situations and behavior that would tempt us to have sex with someone outside of marriage. (1 Cor. 6:18.)

I once had a teenager tell me that the only thing that can truly protect you in sex is a wedding ring. In other words, the only kind of safe sex is saved sex.

God's Word says that our spirit, soul, and body are to be kept strong and blameless until Christ comes back. (1 Thess. 5:23.) A wedding ring (and the lifetime commitment to one mate that it stands for) is the only thing that can protect all three parts of our being from danger.

You see, sex is more than just a physical act that involves your body. It involves your soul and spirit as well. And when you cross that line of intimacy with someone who isn't your husband or wife, you dangerously attach yourself to someone with whom you haven't made a godly covenant through marriage vows.

Believe me, God's plan is the best plan. Stay sexually pure for marriage, because the safest sex of all is the sex you have saved for marriage. Remember, safe sex is saved sex.[40]

make **your** day count

Have you crossed the line where "saved sex" is concerned? If so, ask God to forgive you, so you can once again receive His protection and blessing in your life. Commit to honoring God in your body and saving the gift of sex for your wedding night.

time **saving** tips

Six Reasons to Say "No" to Premarital Sex[41]

Blaine Bartel

The Bible teaches us in 1 Corinthians 6:18 to flee sexual immorality. God is not a "Grinch" trying to steal all the fun out of your teenage years. He wants to protect you and prepare you for a wonderful marriage relationship where sexuality will have its perfect place.

Here are six reasons to say "no" until then.

You will close the door on sin and its destructive nature.

The thought of raising a baby while you're a teenager will never enter your mind.

You will never have a doctor tell you that you've contracted a sexually transmitted disease.

Friends and classmates will never see compromise in your life that will cause them to talk behind your back and lose respect for who you are.

God will be able to trust you with His very best as you give Him your very best.

You will never have to deal with "ghosts of relationships past" in your marriage relationship.

Dirt and Worms

1 bag of gummy worms
1 large and 1 small bag of Oreo cookies, crushed
1 16-oz. Cool Whip
2 8-oz. cream cheese
3 small pkgs. instant vanilla pudding
1 8- or 9-inch flower pot, new and washed clean

Prepare pudding according to directions, except use 4 cups of milk instead of 6.

Add Cool Whip and cream cheese to pudding mixture and blend together.

In the bottom of the flower pot, put a layer of crushed cookies, a few worms, a layer of pudding mixture, a layer of worms, etc., topping it off with a layer of crushed cookies.

Breaking Destructive Soul Ties

Lindsay Roberts

Stand fast therefore in the liberty wherewith Christ hath made us free, and be not entangled again with the yoke of bondage.

—Galatians 5:1 KJV

God has given each of us a spirit and a soul. Your spirit is the part of you that will live forever, even after it leaves your body. Your soul includes your mind, will, emotions, and decision-making processes. God designed the spirit to rule over the soul.

When it comes to the close relationships in your life, you knit your soul to another person's as a relationship grows. You develop a *soul tie* to that person. The danger comes when you knit yourself to someone who is not allowing the Spirit of God to lead them, someone who can pull down your soul so much that they eventually pull down your spirit. *That's a destructive soul tie.*

Perhaps you have left a bad or even abusive relationship, thinking that would end your connection with that person. But until you ask God to help you break that destructive soul tie, that relationship may still be influencing your other relationships and decisions.

God can create a "clean slate" in your soul, freeing you to begin again. Ask God to break any destructive soul ties you have. Then begin renewing your mind with the Word of God. Let the washing of God's Word begin to transform your life as you allow God to speak to your spirit and lead you into new and healthy relationships in Him.[42]

make **your** day count

If you are dealing with a destructive soul tie,
break the power of it right now in Jesus' name.
Determine that only God's thoughts will influence you today.

Backwash

Blaine Bartel

Do not be deceived: God cannot be mocked. A man reaps what he sows. The one who sows to please his sinful nature, from that nature will reap destruction; the one who sows to please the Spirit, from the Spirit will reap eternal life.

—Galatians 6:7,8

While the majority of physically intimate relationships played out on movie and TV screens are between unmarried people, rarely do we see these partners dealing with such consequences as guilt, sexual diseases, or unwanted pregnancy.

Unlike the lives of the characters on the screen, ours can't be fixed with a quick rewrite of a script. When we sow seeds of sin, we will reap a harvest of death. But when we sow seeds of purity, faith, and integrity, we will be able to enjoy a harvest of blessings.

One night at Oneighty®—the youth ministry at my church—I pulled out a can of Coca-Cola and offered a slug to all. It was passed around from one student to another until there was only one gulp left. "Who wants to finish it off?" I asked. Everyone knew what was left: backwash! No one wanted any part of it.

Then I pulled out a fresh can of Coke and said, "Who wants to drink this entire untouched Coke all by yourself?" Students began to scream for the opportunity.

Here was my point. When you guard your body from sexual immorality, one day when you are married you'll be like a fresh can of Coke for your spouse. You won't have to enter the most important relationship of your life polluted with spiritual, emotional, and physical backwash.[43]

make **your** day count

Offering your future mate your physical body is one of the most precious gifts he or she will ever receive. Make the commitment today to preserve that gift for the special day when the two of you will become husband and wife. If you've already shared your gift, receive God's forgiveness today. He can cleanse you and give you a brand-new start.

Seeing Through a Filter

Suzanne Rentz

O taste and see that the Lord is good:
blessed is the man that trusteth in him.

—Psalm 34:8 KJV

Once I went into a store to buy some bread. I was clueless that I was still wearing my sunglasses (which have yellowish-tinted lenses). As I walked down the bread aisle, I couldn't find the usual brand that I buy. All I could find were green bags.

There wasn't a blue package in sight, so I bent down to pick up a green package. As I did, it dawned on me that the package looked green because I was wearing my sunglasses. The tinted lenses changed my perception of the color of the packages.

The bread was right in front of me, yet I didn't see it for what it was because the tint in my sunglasses had changed the truth and the reality of it for me. That is sometimes the way we see ourselves, our future, our lives. But most importantly, that is often the way we see God—through "tinted lenses," or what I call a *filter.* When we see through a filter, things that should make sense sometimes don't.

Do you see God through some kind of filter? The revelation of His unconditional love and acceptance of you is life-changing. Ask Him to reveal any filters that are distorting your view of Him. When you see Him as He is, it will change your life.[44]

make **your** day count

Find Scriptures to counteract any distortions you have of God. For instance, if you think of God as being a hard-to-please, demanding boss, choose to believe what Jesus says instead: "I am gentle and humble in heart.... My yoke is easy and my burden is light" (Matt. 11:29,30).

Virginity Begins in the Mind

Carla Stephens

Those who live according to the flesh set their minds on the things of the flesh, but those who live according to the Spirit, the things of the Spirit. For to be carnally minded is death, but to be spiritually minded is life and peace.

—Romans 8:5,6 NKJV

Virginity begins and ends in your mind, not your body. The same is true for any decision you make for God and against sin. In Genesis 2, God commanded Adam to refrain from eating the fruit of the Tree of the Knowledge of Good and Evil.

The serpent, however, challenged God's motives, thereby planting doubt in the hearts of Adam and Eve. In essence he said, "God lied to you. He knows you won't die. He's just trying to keep you from being like Him. He doesn't want you to have power over your own life."

The purpose of this speech was to push Adam and Eve out of the will of God. The serpent knew that if he could get them to question the validity of God's command, the end result would be their disobedience and sin. Instead of rejecting the serpent's words and trusting in God, Adam and Eve entertained the thoughts the serpent had planted in their minds, resulting in their disobedience.

The same enemy is roaming the earth today, using a variety of methods to plant thoughts in people's minds that contradict God's Word. The more you dwell on these thoughts, the greater will be the urge to act on them.

Don't lose the battle of the mind. Focus on God and His Word and stay committed to sexual purity.[45]

make **your** day count

What thoughts have you been dwelling on? It might help to write them down. Do these thoughts line up with God's Word? Find a favorite passage of Scripture and purposely think about it all day. As you do, your spirit will be strengthened to live a life of purity.

time **saving** tips

What to Say When Someone Is Pressuring You to Have Sex[46]

Pressure line: If you care about me, you'll do it.
Response: If you care about me, you'll respect my feelings and not push me.

Pressure line: If you don't do what I want, I don't want to see you anymore.
Response: If that's the way you feel, I'm not sure I want to see you anymore either.

Pressure line: I know you want to.
Response: If I wanted to, I wouldn't be arguing with you about it.

Pressure line: We're going steady. It's okay.
Response: Going steady doesn't make sex okay for me. Going steady won't prevent pregnancy or stop a disease.

Pressure line: You let me before. Why not now?
Response: It's my body and I have a right to change my mind.

Pressure line: Aren't you curious about it?
Response: Yeah, I'm curious about a lot of things, but that doesn't mean I have to experience them, particularly if I can get hurt.

Pressure line: If you want to be popular, you'll go farther than just kissing.
Response: Who am I going to be popular with, people who want to use me?

Pressure line: But everybody is doing it!
Response: No, they are not. And a lot of the people who do it end up being sorry about it. Besides, I'm not everybody. I know what's right for me.

Peanut Butter and Chocolate Smoothies

Betsy Williams

1 cup milk
2 cups ice
1 tsp. carob or Nestles Quik (or similar product)
1 heaping Tbsp. peanut butter
2 Tbsp. honey
½ frozen banana (remove peel before freezing in a Ziploc bag)

Put all in the blender and let her rip!

You Can Shape Your World

Kenneth Copeland

The tongue has the power of life and death,
and those who love it will eat its fruit.

—Proverbs 18:21

Many Christians think words just communicate information, but words are far more powerful than that. They actually serve as containers for spiritual power. According to the verse above, they carry the power of life and death.

People sometimes speak empty words, but God never does. Every word He has ever spoken has been filled with faith, power, and life. In fact, God's Word actually contains within it the power to do exactly what it says it will do. (Isa. 55:11.)

Every word God has ever spoken is backed by His faith and is as full of power today as it was the moment He said it. So when—by faith—you believe something He has said, the Holy Spirit goes into action, and that Word explodes into this natural realm and becomes a reality in your life!

God's Word can accomplish everything you need: healing, finances, spiritual growth, a job, restored friendships, a new car, better grades, courage. Whatever it is you need, you can speak His promises in faith. Then, as spiritual containers, they will begin to go to work—and what you need will eventually show up right before your eyes. So speak

God's Word, His promises, His words of life and power. You can shape your world![47]

make **your** day count

Be mindful of your words today. Are they filled with faith in God's Word, or are they full of discouragement and fear? Find a Bible promise to counteract an issue you are dealing with and begin speaking it all day long. God spoke the world into existence. You, too, can shape your world. Speak words of life!

When Someone's Baggage Influences Your World

Lindsay Roberts

Let's please the other fellow, not ourselves, and do what is for his good and thus build him up in the Lord.

—Romans 15:2 TLB

Most of us have at least one or two difficult people who seem to rip our peace right out from under us the minute they walk through the door. What do you do when that happens—especially when it's someone close to you?

The Bible tells us that God's love is the key. It's important to remember that the problem isn't the person who is trying to steal your peace. Ephesians 6:12 says, "Our struggle is not against flesh and blood, but against the rulers, against the authorities, against the powers of this dark world and against the spiritual forces of evil in the heavenly realms."

We all know good people with bad baggage. I believe that the spirit of fear is often behind the anxiety and torment people carry in their lives. When their baggage begins to influence your world, your responsibility is to be like God. God is love, so you are to demonstrate the love of God to them.

We must approach these people with love, remembering that the love of God can remove that junk out of their lives.

God will empower you to be patient and kind as you yield yourself to Him. Who knows, you may be just the one God wants to use to bring healing and wholeness to that person.[48]

make **your** day count

Seek out someone whose "baggage" is a challenge to you and purposely bless the person with God's love today.

Keeping Your Heart Safe

Eastman Curtis

There's more to sex than mere skin on skin. Sex is as much spiritual mystery as physical fact. As written in Scripture, "The two become one." Since we want to become spiritually one with the Master, we must not pursue the kind of sex that avoids commitment and intimacy, leaving us more lonely than ever—the kind of sex that can never "become one."

—1 Corinthians 6:16,17 MESSAGE

Unlike so-called "safe sex," saving sex for marriage isn't just to prevent pregnancy. It is to protect your heart from being broken. Sex was made by God to be enjoyed in the context of a covenant marriage relationship. When it is misused outside of marriage, things just won't work out right.

One of the best things you can do today for your future marriage is to decide to stay faithful for your future spouse. That means you pledge to reserve your body for your mate alone—before marriage as well as during marriage. One practical thing you can do to fulfill that commitment is to draw boundary lines for yourself before you ever hold another person's hand. Make godly decisions now—*before* you find yourself in uncomfortable situations where you have to act on those decisions.

God gave us sex with guidelines because He knows we need His guidance in this area. He knows that if we misuse sex, we inevitably heap destruction upon ourselves. We may not see the negative effects of our disobedience right away, but over a period of time, the harvest of destruction in our lives will become evident.

God only wants the best for that covenant relationship you will one day enjoy with your mate. So follow His guidelines, and save sex for marriage.[49]

make **your** day count

Are you willing to make the commitment to save sex for marriage? Even if you've already crossed the line, with God's forgiveness you can start anew. Pray about and write down the physical boundaries you believe will honor God, and make a quality decision to stick with them.

time **saving** tips

More Things to Say When Someone Is Pressuring You to Have Sex[50]

Pressure line: Don't worry, you won't get pregnant or catch a disease.
Response: How do you know? Do you think we're better than any other people?

Pressure line: You got me excited and now you have to do something about it.
Response: I don't have to do anything. I certainly didn't intend to have sex with you. (Hint: You probably won't have this problem if you make it clear that you are practicing abstinence before you go out with someone.)

Pressure line: But I love you.
Response: If you love me, you'll respect my decision.

Pressure line: If you won't do it, I'll find someone who will.
Response: If that's all I mean to you, then find someone else. I wasn't put on earth for you to use.

Pressure line: If I don't relieve this tension, I'll be in pain.
Response: No you won't, that's a myth. Besides, if we do it, we might both be in pain if we get pregnant.

Pressure line: What's wrong with you?
Response: Nothing. Things are right with me. There's nothing wrong with choosing to wait to have sex.

easy **recipes**

Gorp Trail Mix

Betsy Williams

1 large box raisins
1 large bag M&Ms
1 large can cocktail peanuts

Mix all together in a large bowl, then store in an airtight container.

Five Ways to Preserve Virginity

Carla Stephens

Do not let this Book of the Law depart from your mouth; meditate on it day and night, so that you may be careful to do everything written in it. Then you will be prosperous and successful.

—Joshua 1:8

There are five ways to fortify our minds and therefore, preserve our virginity.

1. Meditate on God's Word—ponder or dwell upon it. Then the doubt, fear, and disbelief the devil tries to plant in our minds will disintegrate because that space is already taken up with God's Word. Every thought we dwell on ultimately results in action, whether positive or negative.
2. Consistently spend time in God's Word. Every time we choose not to spend consistent quality time with God, we give the enemy entrance into our lives.
3. Obey the Word. It is the way we show we love Him. The more we obey, the more He showers His blessings upon us.
4. Resist peer pressure. We must be careful whom we hang out with because evil companionships will bring us down. (1 Cor. 15:33.) The best cure for peer

pressure is the confidence that comes from knowing that God has a plan for your life. (Jer. 29:11.)

5. Practice the presence of God, which simply means become aware of the heavenly audience watching you. (Heb. 12:1.) Whatever we do in secret or in the dark can always be seen by those in that heavenly audience, especially God.

Doing these things will help us avoid dwelling on the thoughts that may cause us to fall away from God's will for our lives.[51]

make **your** day count

Look up the Scriptures stated above as well as James 4:7.
Write these verses down and ponder them all day today.
Let your last thoughts before you drop off to sleep be about those verses.

The Final Frontier

Gloria Copeland

Just as he who called you is holy, so be holy in all you do.

—1 Peter 1:15

Today we are standing at the edge of a great frontier. I believe it is the final frontier that stands between us and the greatest move of God this earth has ever seen. What is the last great, spiritual frontier?

Holiness.

That's right. Holiness is the final frontier, and we will cross it before Jesus returns. I know we will because the Bible says that He is coming for a Church without spot or wrinkle. (Eph. 5:27.) In other words, He is coming for a Church that is holy.

Holiness is what allows God's power to explode in the earth. The more we walk in holiness, the more God will be able to touch the world and show Himself through us! In fact, that's what holiness is. It simply means "being separated to God for His use."

Knowing that should make us hunger for holiness. It should make us more eager than ever to separate ourselves from worldly things and make godly things the biggest part of our lives.

So commit yourself to being holy. Give yourself completely over to God for His use. Then get ready to see God's power explode in your youth group, your school, your workplace, and your home. Get ready to cross the final frontier![52]

make **your** day count

What things are a hindrance to your life of faith and holiness? Take them to God in prayer and lay them at His feet today. As you let go of worldly things and grab hold of God, He will be free to work in your life. He has an amazing life of adventure planned for you!

Be a Risk-Taker

Blaine Bartel

If you wait for perfect conditions,
you will never get anything done.
—Ecclesiastes 11:4 TLB

We have all heard people tell us to "play it safe" in life. But the ones who experience great success in life are those who take the right risks.

In baseball, Babe Ruth held the record for the most home runs, but he also held the record for the most strikeouts. Why? Because he didn't play it safe. He didn't try for a single or double when he was at bat. When he was swinging, it was for a home run. He swung so hard, one of two things was going to happen. Either he was going to miss, which only meant he could take another try, or he was going to knock the ball out of the park.

When life pitches you the ball, you can play it safe and wait for the perfect pitch, which rarely comes, or you can increase your chances of hitting it out of the park by swinging more and waiting less.

Do you have a dream for a career that seems too big, and are you tempted to shoot for less because you're afraid to fail? Do you want to witness to a friend but fear striking out, so you don't try? Those who are inducted into life's hall of fame are not the ones who play it safe; they play to win.

Swing at your dreams. You just might surprise yourself with a home run. You will never know until you try.[53]

make **your** day count

What is that thing in your life that you would go for if you knew you could not fail? Talk to God about that thing today and take a step of faith toward accomplishing your dream.

God Likes You

Suzanne Rentz

The Lord your God...
will rejoice over you with gladness,
He will quiet you with His love,
He will rejoice over you with singing.
—Zephaniah 3:17 NKJV

Did you know that God *likes* you? That may sound strange, because we're so used to hearing that God *loves* us, but He not only loves you; He *likes* you!

Recently, I had a picture taken for a brochure. Afterward, the photographer said, "Did you know we can change the background?" I said, "Maybe that would be better." So we started looking at his selections.

After that, I asked if he could smooth out the wrinkles on my face, which he did. Then I said, "My teeth don't look very white," and he then proceeded to whiten them in the picture. Then, I said, "What about fixing my eyes?" We finally stopped touching up the photo when I asked him to give me highlights in my hair, which made me look as if I had fuzzy skunk hair. The more I stared at my picture and tried to change it, the more I didn't like it and the more I saw my flaws.

What an illustration of the way we often look at our own lives. When we don't look at our lives through God's eyes, we try and perfect what we think are flaws in ourselves. The truth is that your Father God created you, and in His eyes you are perfect. Remember, He not only loves you, He *likes* you.[54]

make **your** day count

Instead of wasting time and energy thinking about your flaws today—in whatever area—think about how crazy God is about you. He created you and He thinks you are awesome in every way. Ask Him to help you see yourself the way He does.

time **saving** tips

Seven Ways to Avoid Premarital Sex[55]

Blaine Bartel

It's one thing to know that we should flee sexual immorality, but you may be wondering, "How do I do it?" Here are seven ways that you can avoid the sin that can destroy you and your future.

Sexual sin starts in the mind, so win the war there first by studying the Bible. Fill your mind with God's Word.

Stay in church. The more you hear the Word and stay close to other Christians, the better you will keep your focus on spiritual things.

Don't ever go out alone with a person you know will tempt you or easily give in to sexual sin.

Don't allow yourself to be alone with the opposite sex in a place where temptation is easily fostered.

Stay away from sexually suggestive books, magazines, photos, or Web sites that will stir up sexual desires.

Build relationships of accountability with parents and strong Christian friends. When going through a trying time, let them know and ask for their help.

Make up your mind. Never retreat. Let every new friend you meet know you are committed to sexual purity.

easy **recipes**

Fruit Smoothies

Betsy Williams

2 oz. pineapple or apple juice
½ frozen banana (remove peel before freezing in a Ziploc bag)
4 pieces frozen fruit such as strawberries, peaches, or a handful of blueberries
2 Tbsp. honey
2 cups crushed ice

Blend all ingredients in blender until smooth.

Don't Strut Your Stuff

Kate McVeigh

I also want women to dress modestly, with decency and propriety, not with braided hair or gold or pearls or expensive clothes, but with good deeds, appropriate for women who profess to worship God.

—1 Timothy 2:9,10

One time my brother and I were discussing sexual temptation and how hard it is for men to stay pure when women dress seductively. He told me about a time when he and some friends were waiting in line at a restaurant. A woman walked by them whose clothes were so tight that she didn't leave much to the imagination. She walked by this group really "strutting her stuff."

Immediately every man's head turned toward her as she walked by. When she saw them staring, she stopped and looked at all the men with a disgusting look, as if to say, "What are you staring at?" So my brother said to her, "If you don't want us staring at your body, then don't put it on display!" That was a bit bold, but he was right.

Sometimes women dress that way because they're insecure and want attention. But they don't realize the message they are sending. As Christians, we don't have to dress or act like the world. We can still be "in" without compromising.

Scripture makes it clear that we should dress modestly. Christian women can look beautiful without being seductive.

Just be careful about what message you are sending. Don't make it even harder on men to resist temptation. Make it easier for them, and save yourself for the right one.[56]

make **your** day count

Is there anything seductive about the clothes you wear or the way you act? If so, get to the root of why. What need are you trying to fulfill? Next, go to God and repent. Ask Him to show you how to get that need met in a godly way. If change is needed, make that change today.

If My People Will Pray

Lindsay Roberts

If my people, who are called by my name, will humble themselves and pray and seek my face and turn from their wicked ways, then will I hear from heaven and will forgive their sin and will heal their land.

—2 Chronicles 7:14

I believe that we can start a worldwide revival…today! And one way we can do it and bring peace in the midst of chaos is to humble ourselves and pray. Notice that God wasn't talking about the devil's crowd! He said, "If *my* people…."

In the rest of the sentence, He says, "and turn from their wicked ways." We've got sin in our lives, and if we want God to heal us, we need to fall on our faces before God and repent. Instead of spending your days watching some ungodly program or video, consider spending time on your knees before the face of an awesome and powerful God.

The time has come when we've got to be in a place of prayer and a place of prayer covering. These are dangerous times, and we *have* to have a Power Source greater than this world. That Source is Jesus Christ of Nazareth, the Prince of Peace, King of kings, and Lord of lords.

I believe God is calling us together as a body of believers to get the garbage out of our lives. Because when we do, the Holy Spirit of God can rise up inside of us, and we can be a beacon of light to a dark and troubled world. We sing about being a light in darkness. Now let's do it![57]

make **your** day count

Even if it is only five or ten minutes, take some time today to humble yourself, make sure your heart is right before God, and pray for our nation.

No Comparison

Eastman Curtis

If you harbor bitter envy and selfish ambition in your hearts, do not boast about it or deny the truth. Such "wisdom" does not come down from heaven but is earthly, unspiritual, of the devil. For where you have envy and selfish ambition, there you find disorder and every evil practice.

—James 3:14–16

Comparing ourselves with others may seem innocent enough, but it can sometimes grow into an ugly monster of jealousy. At first we may feel as if we are doing pretty well and are somewhere near "the top of the stack." But eventually we come to realize that we may not be quite as good as someone else in a particular area. We begin to feel as if we are closer to the bottom of the stack than we realized. Slowly, our character becomes poisoned with envy. Soon we become so infected that it's hard to remember what we ever liked about ourselves. This jealousy can destroy us if we let it.

Sure, there may be someone who does some things better than you do, but that's okay. You just need to accept that fact and realize that God has given you special gifts and talents as well, even though they may be in totally different areas.

So find out what your particular gifts are and focus on them. Allow Christ to develop you into the unique person He created you to be. Once you realize that Jesus has already purchased and given you every good thing you could ever need to accomplish what He has called you to do, you won't be so tempted to drink the poisonous wine of jealousy.[58]

make **your** day count

Have you been comparing yourself to others? Write down your three greatest strengths. Thank God for them and ask Him to show you how at least one of those strengths can be used by Him today. Then step out and do it.

time **saving** tips

Eight Goals to Reach Before You're Eighteen[59]

Blaine Bartel

At every stage in life, it is important to learn to set incremental goals towards the fulfillment of your dreams and vision. I encourage you to write your goals down as a regular reference point for your progress. Here are eight goals to consider attaining before you're eighteen.

Make a long-term financial investment in the stock market.

Read the Bible through entirely.

Hold down one job for at least six months—a year if possible.

Read Dale Carnegie's book, How to Win Friends and Influence People.

Obtain a basic idea of what career direction you are going to take, and make the necessary plans for school or training.

Develop one strong friendship that you will keep for life, no matter where you both end up.

Save enough money to buy a decent used car.

Keep your grades up, and get your high school diploma.

easy **recipes**

Christmas Wreaths[60]

6 12-oz. bars white chocolate
Small bag pretzels
1 bag red shoestring licorice
1 bag sprinkles

Melt chocolate in double boiler on top of the stove or in a glass bowl or measuring cup in the microwave. Can use pan on stovetop on low temperature if very careful to not let the chocolate stick, scorch, or burn.

Dip pretzels in chocolate, then dip in sprinkles.

Place in a circle on waxed paper to dry.

Thread licorice (like a shoestring) through several pretzels to make a wreath.

Make a bow with one string of licorice and place it at the top of the pretzel wreath.

You can also tie a bow on individual pretzels and hang them on your Christmas tree.

Love Yourself

Blaine Bartel

Jesus said, "Love your neighbor as yourself."

—Matthew 19:19

The Bible commands each of us to love his neighbor as he loves himself. This instruction begins with the foundation of loving ourselves first. That would be "me." I am not talking about developing an attitude of selfishness, but rather about learning to operate with a healthy self-esteem.

It is important that you highly esteem the person God has made you and greatly value what He has called you to do. A holy confidence will enable you to relate more effectively with those around you.

I am well-known among my friends and family for letting my car run out of gas. I'm always pushing the fuel tank to its limit, and sometimes I end up on the side of the road waiting for my wife, Cathy, to show up with a can of gas.

The love of God is a critical fuel in your life. You can't give someone else something that you don't have. You must love yourself with God's love before you'll ever be able to really love someone else. That simply means that you need to respect all that God has put inside you and choose His best for your life at all times.

Stop running on empty. Choose to receive all that God wants to fill you with.[61]

make **your** day count

How are you doing at loving yourself? Pray the prayer in Ephesians 3:17–19, asking God to reveal His awesome love for you. Next, make the decision to accept and love yourself. God doesn't make any junk!

A True Reflection

Marty Copeland

The Lord does not look at the things man looks at.
Man looks at the outward appearance,
but the Lord looks at the heart.

—1 Samuel 16:7

When I was growing up, I was overweight and obsessed with dieting and exercise. The world told me that my value was based on my appearance. I put way too much emphasis on my outside appearance and not nearly enough on the inside. So God had to straighten out my thinking. Our quest should not be to look great on the outside, but we should wake up and ask, "Father, how can I be a good reflection of Your character today?"

Whether we like it or not, our bodies send a message to other people. That's why I believe that taking good care of our bodies is not about vanity but about being a representative of God. Most people are not as interested in hearing us teach the Bible as they are in watching how we conduct our lives.

I understand the torment of struggling with weight, but God wants us to be free from *any* form of bondage. If we set our purpose on His purpose—which is to reflect His character in order to draw others to Him—then I believe there is supernatural power to help us get our bodies into shape.

First Corinthians 6:19 says that our bodies are the temples of the Holy Spirit. We can honor our temples by taking good care of them, and God can help us![62]

make **your** day count

Make an investment in your spirit by spending a few minutes reading God's Word and talking to Him. Then make an investment in your body by eating an extra fruit and an extra vegetable. Last, do some form of exercise, even if it's just walking around the block.

Stay Connected

Gloria Copeland

Jesus said, "Here I am! I stand at the door and knock.
If anyone hears my voice and opens the door,
I will come in and eat with him, and he with me."

—Revelation 3:20

Wouldn't life be wonderfully simple if there was only one thing that truly mattered or determined your success? Instead of constantly juggling priorities, you'd always know what to put first.

There is, in fact, only one real key to victory in life—a continual connection with God.

In years past, I used to say, "If things aren't going well, check to see if you're walking in love." Or, "If you're not getting your prayers answered, make sure you aren't harboring any unforgiveness." I had learned that by checking those spiritual gauges, you could track down the causes for failure.

Even though such gauges are very helpful, I've come to realize that ultimately our success stems solely from our continual contact with God. Then those other qualities will flow naturally from you. You will walk in love, joy, and forgiveness.

So what exactly is a continual connection with God? It simply means keeping the lines of communication open between the two of you. It means going about your daily activities in such a way that you're always ready to hear from Him.

Just think: The real key to consistent victory is just one thing! You don't have to memorize a list of do's and don'ts. All you have to do is stay in continual contact with God and keep your ear tuned to Him.[63]

make **your** day count

Make it a point to spend time talking to God today. Invite Him into every activity and conversation. At the same time, keep your ear open to hear His voice. He wants to help you succeed and He knows what you need to do to get there. Listen to His voice, then promptly obey. You cannot fail when you obey God.

He Will Guide You Through

Suzanne Rentz

He tends his flock like a shepherd:
He gathers the lambs in his arms
and carries them close to his heart.

—Isaiah 40:11

God desires to be a part of your life. If you sang for the first time in front of a group of people, He was right there saying, "That's my girl." If your friend betrayed you and you felt crushed and broken, your Father God saw that and hurt for you.

I love that God is El Roi, "the God who sees" (Gen. 16:13). He's the God who knows everything, and He still loves us intimately. He wants us to tell Him what's going on and how we feel.

There are times when I'm upset and I tell Him the whole situation. There are times when I'm really scared about things, but I've learned to stretch out my hand and say, "Father God, hold my hand and walk me through this. I can't make it without You, but with You, I can do all things." (Phil. 4:13.) It's just like a little girl with so many things all over her room that she can't see the way to walk out of it. Then her dad comes, takes her by the hand, and says, "Come on, I'll guide you through."

Every time I feel insecure or scared, or when circumstances seem out of control, I hold His hand. The best part is that I know He holds me. And He holds you too.[64]

make **your** day count

Reach out your hand to God today and call out to Him. He will hold your hand as you face each and every circumstance today. Think about the fact that He's there with you, comforting you, helping you, cheering you on. Then be sure to praise Him for His goodness and faithfulness to you.

time **saving** tips

Things to Learn Before You Move Away from Home

The time eventually comes for most teens to move into a dorm or apartment of their own. There are a few basic things you should know. Learn how to:

Cook simple things like oatmeal and boil an egg. Follow simple recipes. Use a microwave oven, gas and electric stoves, toaster oven, blender, mixer, and Crock-Pot.

Shop for groceries and household items. Figure the cost per unit to get the best deal—largest isn't always the best value.

Do laundry and operate a washing machine and dryer.

Check the fluid levels in your car and know when to add more fluid. Learn the color of each vital fluid and how to check for leaks. Get a car maintenance schedule. Know how to check air pressure in tires and inflate to proper level.

Balance your checkbook.

Fill out a job application. Prepare a résumé. Compile list of references with complete contact information.

Set up a budget. Pay bills on time. Understand debt and why to avoid it.

Schedule annual physicals and teeth cleanings.

easy **recipes**

Peanut-Butter Balls

Betsy Williams

1/2 cup margarine
1/2 cup light Karo syrup
3/4 cup peanut butter, smooth or chunky
1/2 tsp. salt
1 tsp. vanilla
4 cups sifted powdered sugar

Mix together margarine, Karo syrup, and peanut butter.

Sift salt and powdered sugar, and add gradually to peanut butter mixture.

Add vanilla and blend well.

Form into small balls and let stand until firm.

You can also dip these in melted milk chocolate.

What Are You Filling Up On?

Lindsay Roberts

Above all else, guard your heart,
for it affects everything you do.
—Proverbs 4:23 NLT

It is vitally important what we put into our spirits. Because of the society we live in, we can watch movies that are filled with lust, curse words, and pornography. No matter how nicely they try to put it, little to no clothing on people slides into the category of pornography. And when we take all of that into our spirits, we become open to those sinful influences.

Over time we become desensitized to evil. We open our spirits to all the turmoil of the world, because as Christians we don't stop it. And not only do we not stop it, but we *embrace* it by the fact that we watch it and even pay to be entertained by it.

Did you know that the word *video* comes from the Latin word meaning "to envy" or "be jealous"? What are you watching? What videos games are you playing? What are you watching on the Internet?

You know, many Christians are well educated, well dressed, well behaved. They declare Christianity with their mouths, but live lifestyles that speak otherwise. First, we have to repent of the garbage and degradation we've allowed into our lives. Then we must vigilantly guard our hearts, so the life of God can flow freely in and through us.[65]

make **your** day count

Be especially mindful today of the things you allow your eyes to see and your ears to hear. Fill them with the good things of God's Word.

Getting Along with Stepparents

Eastman Curtis

If someone claims, "I know him [God] well!" but doesn't keep his commandments, he's obviously a liar. His life doesn't match his words. But the one who keeps God's word is the person in whom we see God's mature love. This is the only way to be sure we're in God. Anyone who claims to be intimate with God ought to live the same kind of life Jesus lived.

—1 John 2:3–6 MESSAGE

I can tell you from experience that stepparents can be a brand-new challenge in life. In fact, I remember well the time when—right in the middle of working through all the emotions I had as a result of my parents' divorce—I had to turn around and readjust to brand-new parents.

That experience can be a stretch to your love walk, but God's love in you can prevail. Here are some things that will make it easier for you to adjust to stepparents:

First, show your stepparents respect. Real respect translates into love. I am talking about real love—active love that makes a difference. As you determine in your heart to show this kind of love, God will help develop it in you.

Second, try to remember that it is just as much of a stretch for your stepparents to adjust to you as it is for you to adjust to them. It may be hard to see it from their perspective at first, but at least try to put yourself in their place and understand what they may be dealing with.

With God's help and your decision to walk in love, a great relationship is bound to begin between you and your stepparents.[66]

make **your** day count

If you have a stepparent, think of something you could do to reflect God's love to him or her today, then pray for God to bless your stepparent. If you don't have a stepparent, but you have a friend who does, pray for the relationship between your friend and his or her stepparent.

"Unreasonable" Christianity

Blaine Bartel

Don't become so well-adjusted to your culture that you fit into it without even thinking. Instead, fix your attention on God. You'll be changed from the inside out. Readily recognize what he wants from you, and quickly respond to it.
—Romans 12:2 MESSAGE

George Bernard Shaw wrote, "A reasonable man adapts himself to the world around him. An unreasonable man expects the world to adapt to him. Therefore, all progress is made by unreasonable men."

Mr. Shaw is echoing the Scripture above that encourages us to avoid conforming to the world's mold. I call this unreasonable Christianity.

Martin Luther was one such "unreasonable" Christian. He was shocked by the corruption in the church in his day. The religious hierarchy demanded money and penance from the people who wanted forgiveness. According to their traditions, prayers were to be given to God through the mediator of a priest.

Instead of going with the flow, Luther went to Whittenburg castle and nailed a ninety-five-point thesis on a wooden door. The core truth was that every believer is justified by personal faith in God—not by works. He launched the great Reformation and eventually suffered excommunication and public condemnation from the church. But Martin Luther was fully persuaded that holding fast to the Word of God was far more important than the acceptance of his peers.

Reason will tell you that if everyone else in your school is doing drugs and having sex, then there's nothing wrong with your doing the same. It's time to be unreasonable. Changing your thoughts will change your actions. Changing your actions will change the world.[67]

make **your** day count

Is there an area in which you need to become "unreasonable"?
If you aren't sure, turn to the Bible for answers.
Then, don't just go with the flow. Be a world-changer!

time **saving** tips

Five Ways to Get a Great Job[68]

Blaine Bartel

Get out into the workplace and hunt your job down. Knock on doors, set up interviews, and learn to sell your desire and ability.

Be sure you have properly trained and prepared yourself for the job you really want. If it means college, find a way to get to college. Read, learn, intern, volunteer, and do whatever it takes to become the best in your field.

Start out in any company or organization being willing to do the small things that other "big shots" aren't willing to do. It will separate and distinguish you from the pack.

Set your sights high. Don't allow your own self-doubt or other people's lack of support stop you from going after your goals. (Mark 11:24.)

Pray and trust God to open up the doors supernaturally. He can, and He will. (Jer. 33:3.)

easy **recipes**

Beenie Weenies

Betsy Williams

1 package of hot dogs
1 can (1 lb. 15 oz.) pork and beans
⅓ cup brown sugar

Cut hot dogs into bite-sized chunks.

Put all ingredients in Crock-Pot and cook on high for 1–2 hours.

You Are God's Favorite Child

Kate McVeigh

You, O Lord, will bless the righteous; with favor
You will surround him as with a shield.

—Psalm 5:12 NKJV

You are God's favorite child. This revelation transformed my life. I have so much favor operating in my life now that I believe I'm God's favorite child. When His favor begins to manifest and you see Him do so many good things in your life, you can't help but believe that you must be His absolute favorite child. (Deut. 32:9,10; Matt. 7:11.)

I believe that one day of favor is worth a thousand days of labor. God can do for you in one day what could take years to accomplish alone. Notice in our text verse that the Lord will bless us—the righteous in Christ—with favor.

To be *favored* means "(1) regarded or treated with favor; specif., (a) provided with advantages…specially privileged…."[69] God wants to give you special privileges. The favor of God causes people to go out of their way to bless you without knowing why, whether they like you or not.

We should believe God for favor on a daily basis. Every morning in the shower I confess favor around my life. It surrounds me like a shield. You would be amazed if you knew all the miraculous blessings I have received because of that favor. If you are a believer, you also have been made righteous in Christ, and that same favor that blesses me will bless you too.[70]

make **your** day count

Look up the verses used above and claim God's promise that favor surrounds you as a shield today. God wants you to have all of the advantages and privileges that His favor provides. Don't settle for anything less!

Untouchable

Kim Freeman

Jesus said, "I will not speak with you much longer, for the prince of this world is coming. He has no hold on me."

—John 14:30

Years ago, there was a television program called *The Untouchables.* It centered around the gangsters of the Capone era and the government agents who sought to bring them to justice.

The basis of the series was that although corruption was rampant in the law enforcement community, one special group of government agents had come to be regarded as "The Untouchables." They were morally clean—couldn't be bought. There was nothing in them that gave their enemies access into their lives.

You could say that Jesus was untouchable, as the verse above indicates. He never allowed sin to have a place in His life. As a result, the devil had no authority over Him.

Because of what Jesus accomplished by sacrificing Himself for us, the same can be said of every believer today—the devil has no authority over us. The problem is that when we sin, we open the door to the enemy, giving him permission to invade our lives. Sin is like a magnet to the devil. It attracts him to us and gives him legitimate access into our lives.

Have we left a door open for the devil somewhere? If so, it's time to cut off his supply lines. It's time to start living the kind of life that will enable us to say, "The devil has nothing in me."[71]

make **your** day count

As you read this devotion, are you aware of an area of your life in which you've given access to the devil through disobedience or sin? If so, confess it to God, receive His forgiveness, and once and for all, shut the door of your life to the devil.

Sheltered by the Rock

Suzanne Rentz

In the day of trouble
he will keep me safe in his dwelling;
he will hide me in the shelter of his tabernacle
and set me high upon a rock.
—Psalm 27:5

God is our Rock. When our world is shaken, He is still our Rock; He is our Foundation. Psalm 91 describes God as being our shelter. That means you can run to Him and He is there for you. When you face huge disappointments, when people fail you (and they will) and when circumstances are out of control (and they will be at times), when it's foggy and you can't see where to step next, the one thing you can be sure of is that your Father God will remain unchanged. He will always be your firm Foundation, your strong Tower, your Refuge from the storms of life. If you remember nothing else, remember that you can always put your feet on the Foundation (of His Word), and you will not fall.

Sometimes I think we give up on ourselves. We think, *I have failed too many times, and I am not going to repent anymore because I'll probably fail again.* You know what? Your heavenly Father believes in you when you don't believe in yourself, when you can't believe in yourself, when you think you've lost it all. He's right there saying, "I believe in you. Let's try again."

He'll never give up on you. He'll always be there believing in you, knowing that you can make it with His help.[72]

make **your** day count

Regardless of what you did or did not do yesterday or the day before, receive God's courage to try again today. He doesn't expect you to do it on your own, but He is reaching out to you with His grace. Receive that grace by faith today, and step out once again.

Toxic Strife

Gloria Copeland

Let nothing be done through strife or vainglory; but in lowliness of mind let each esteem other better than themselves.

—Philippians 2:3 KJV

One of the most toxic weapons Satan uses against us is *strife*—vigorous or bitter conflict; to quarrel, clash; competition; rivalry. Strife gives Satan the license to bring trouble into your life. That's why he's always pushing for us to argue with one another and get offended or critical. It gives him access to our lives!

When you made Jesus your Lord, the Bible says you were rescued out of the control of darkness. (Col. 1:13.) Right then, Satan lost his right of lordship over you. Salvation doesn't just include going to Heaven. It includes all kinds of benefits on earth too, like peace, healing, well-being, and help for every area of your life.

Satan doesn't want you to enjoy those things. He doesn't want you to be peaceful and healed and happy, because if you are, other people will notice and want what you have. They'll want God.

In order to stop that from happening, Satan tries to steal those things from you, but since he has no rule over you anymore, he has to trick you into opening your life to him. So he tries to get you into strife.

Don't let Satan into your life. Put strife out of your life. Put it out of your family. Put it out of your friendships. When you do, you'll enjoy life like never before![73]

make **your** day count

Is there someone with whom you are tempted to get into strife? Someone in your family? Someone at school or work? Make the commitment to forgive that person today and walk in love toward him or her. The price for strife just isn't worth it. Besides, love never fails!

time **saving** tips

Ideas for Teen Parties

Betsy Williams

Taco party. Go with a Hispanic theme, including a piñata. Have everyone wear a sombrero and bring all the fixings for a taco dinner. Include chips, salsa, black olives, chili con queso, and guacamole among the things your guests bring.

Make-your-own-pizza party. Purchase pizza crusts and pizza sauce. Have your guests bring all the toppings. You could purchase small pizza crusts so that everyone has their own. Give awards for the most original and tastiest pizzas.

Ice cream party. Everyone brings a topping, cones, or ice cream.

Girls only: have a makeover party. The girls could give each other facials and makeovers or invite an Avon or Mary Kay consultant. Take before-and-after photos.

Hawaiian luau: Have everyone dress in Hawaiian shirts. Give all the guests leis; inexpensive ones can be purchased at a party shop. Play Beach Boys or tropical music. (Check your local library; they loan music for free.) Have a limbo contest and give the winner a bobble-head hula dancer or some other prize that fits the theme.

Pick a decade and have everyone dress in attire from that era—such as a "Rock Around the Clock" fifties party or a "Flower Power" sixties party—and play the top hits from that time period.

easy **recipes**

Awesome Garlic Cheese Toast

Betsy Williams

This bread is great as a snack or to serve with spaghetti or any Italian dish. You can cook the whole loaf at once or just a few pieces as you want them.

1 loaf of French bread. Sourdough is best. You can usually buy it already sliced, which saves time.

1 stick of butter softened (can use margarine)

Garlic powder (*not* garlic salt)

1 pkg. grated Parmesan cheese (not the kind in the can, but the kind in the plastic pouch)

Spread however many slices you want onto a cookie sheet, face up.

Spread softened butter on each slice.

Sprinkle garlic powder on each slice.

Top with the Parmesan cheese.

Broil (not bake) in the oven, watching closely to make sure it doesn't burn. Just broil long enough to brown it a bit.

Making Wise Choices

Eastman Curtis

Wisdom will enter your heart,
and knowledge will be pleasant to your soul.
Discretion will protect you,
and understanding will guard you.
Wisdom will save you from the ways of wicked men.
—Proverbs 2:10–12

God loves us so much that He wants us all to enjoy the blessings that are found in His Word. But He didn't create us to be robots, and He doesn't make our choices for us. I just thank God for young adults who want to make wise choices. Unfortunately, many have good intentions but never follow through because of peer pressure and temptation.

It is either our choices or the choices of others that lead us into suffering. The good news is that you are loved with an everlasting love and God already has made a way for you to enjoy total peace and safety through Jesus Christ.

You can take a few simple steps to increase the likelihood that you will make wise choices. First of all, only hang around people who are good influences. Don't make temptation and peer pressure stronger forces than they already are.

Also, stay away from those who say one thing and then do another. People like that are liars and are likely to get you into trouble.

Then finally—and this is so important—make your decisions before you get into tempting situations. Make it known that you don't drink and that you don't go to parties. Then it will be a whole lot easier to turn down those invitations if they come. Remember, the decisions of tomorrow are made with the heart today.[75]

make **your** day count

Think about your friends. Who has a good influence over you? Who has a bad one? Make a good choice today by spending time with a friend who will encourage your walk with God.

Meditating on God's Word

Sarah Bowling

His delight is in the law of the Lord,
and on his law he meditates day and night.
He is like a tree planted by streams of water,
which yields its fruit in season
and whose leaf does not wither.
Whatever he does prospers.

—Psalm 1:2,3

The kind of meditation the Bible speaks of is not Eastern-style meditation. It's not about disengaging the mind and letting it take you where it will. It's about engaging your mind and precisely focusing it on God's Word.

Bible meditation is much like the process a cow uses in digesting her food. Cows have two stomachs. Initially, they chew their food and it goes into the first stomach to be digested so the nutrients can be absorbed. Then the cow regurgitates her digested food, chews on it some more, and then swallows it into the second stomach. There even more nutrients are squeezed out of the food.

When you meditate on the Word of God, you take it into your mind. As you memorize the verses and meditate on them, you gain certain insights. When you go on to other things, your subconscious mind is still "chewing" on the verses. When you go back to your verses for further study and meditation, you bring them back to your mind (or "regurgitate" them) and gain even more insight. Eventually, the verses are "swallowed" into your heart and become a part of you. "You are what you eat." Those Scriptures will continue to speak to you long after you've moved on to meditate on and memorize other verses.[76]

make **your** day count

Write down a Scripture on an index card and take it with you everywhere you go today. In your spare moments, pull out the card and think about the verse. Say it to yourself. Finally, read it before you go to sleep tonight. Your spirit and soul will continue to "digest" that verse even while you sleep.

time **saving** tips

Five Questions Real Friends Should Ask Each Other[77]

Blaine Bartel

A smart person is known by the good questions he or she asks. When Jesus was twelve years old, He was found in the temple asking questions of the teachers of the law.

Here are five questions that good friends should ask of good friends:

How can I be a better friend to you?

Are there any traits, attitudes, or actions you see in my life that hinder my success?

What gifts and characteristics do you recognize as strengths in my life?

How can I pray for you at this time in your life?

What has God shown you in His Word lately?

easy **recipes**

Chocolate-Dipped Pretzels and Oreo's®

Betsy Williams

These make great gifts for Christmas, Valentine's Day, birthdays, or any occasion.

3 pkgs. almond bark or 3 pkgs. milk chocolate bark
1 large bag pretzels, not the straight stick kind
1 bag of Oreos
Sprinkles or drizzle icing, colors based on gift-giving occasion

Melt either the almond or dark chocolate bark according to package instructions. Can use double boiler on top of the stove or a large glass bowl or measuring cup in the microwave. Double boiler is best because the chocolate doesn't cool off and solidify like it does if you melt it in the microwave. Do *not* melt in a regular pan on top of stove; can easily stick, scorch, or burn.

One by one, dip the pretzels or Oreos into the melted chocolate and put on waxed paper to harden.

Before they harden, decorate with sprinkles or colored icing drizzled on them.

Give the pretzels and/or Oreos in a decorative tin or jar.

Making Friends

Blaine Bartel

A man that hath friends must show himself friendly: and there is a friend that sticketh closer than a brother.

—Proverbs 18:24 KJV

I'll never forget the very first youth group I pastored. There was a girl who was always so sad and depressed. She would just stand in the corner of the room by herself before and after each meeting.

One night she came up to me and said, "Pastor Blaine, nobody in this youth group likes me. They're not very friendly."

She had absolutely never made any attempt to talk to anyone. She always looked so mean and depressed that most were afraid to even approach her. I told her that she—not everyone else—was the problem.

"Put a smile on your face. Introduce yourself. Take an interest in others. Friends will follow," I told her.

On the other hand, we once had a really odd-looking young man in our youth group. He was a happy, outgoing, friendly young man and had girls constantly vying for his attention. All the other guys who thought they were better looking than he couldn't figure it out.

The world says looks, image, and beauty are the highest priorities in relating to one another; but in truth good character and the fruit of the Spirit are what will make you attractive to others. Kindness is what makes you desirable to be around.[78]

make **your** day count

How do you come across to others? Determine to smile and speak to everyone you see today. A smile from you will inspire smiles from others. People like to be around those who make them feel good.

"I Say Live!"

Suzanne Rentz

I made you grow like a plant of the field. You grew up and developed and became the most beautiful of jewels.
—Ezekiel 16:7

Ezekiel 16 tells a story that I believe illustrates how much your heavenly Father loves you. One day a prince was walking when he saw something on the ground up ahead.[79] To his great surprise, he found a newborn baby who was flailing and kicking. There was life left in her, but blood was everywhere. She had been left to die, yet she was holding on to life.

The prince picked her up and said, "I don't care where you're from or who left you here to die. When others say die, I say live."

There is death screaming at you from every angle—in music, movies, books, magazines, and on television and the Internet. Death and hopelessness are everywhere. But God says live! Society's perception of the truth warps the mind and cloaks the eyes from the true hunger of the heart—to be loved and accepted and live a life of freedom, happiness, and contentment. That comes from being empowered with God's Word and walking in His presence.

You may feel as though you don't have any kick left, but God sees you right where you are, just as the prince saw that helpless baby. God wants to pick you up and let you experience His love. He is ready to move in your life and turn the tide from destruction to restoration.[80]

make **your** day count

You don't have to carry pain in your heart today. The book of Psalms is filled with words that most likely describe you, whatever your heart is feeling. Find one that you can relate to and let God comfort You with His Word today.

Three Things God Has Given You

Sarah Bowling

The Lord God formed the man from the dust of the ground and breathed into his nostrils the breath of life, and the man became a living being.

—Genesis 2:7

In Genesis 1 when God creates the world, He uses the term *Elohim* for Himself. The almighty God who made the universe knit you together. In Genesis 2 when God begins to describe the fashioning of man, He changes his name to *Jehovah,* which means the personal God.[81] He is both almighty and personal. He made you for relationship with Him.

First, you are made in His image. When you understand that you are made in the image of God, that you have His essential nature, it takes you from a mere base mammal existence and places you on a higher level.

Second, God has given you distinction. You are unique. Even if you don't like yourself, God likes you. He's absolutely crazy about you. He designed you so that He could have a relationship with you.

Third, you have the breath of the Almighty within you. The breath of the Almighty transcends time, people, ethnicity, and language—every imaginable difference among humanity.

When you begin to truly understand that God is your Author, He is your Father, it changes everything. You should have an identity crisis. Get rid of the garbage that limits you and receive your true identity so that you can implement your purpose. Your true Father, your true Creator, is not your earthly father, but your heavenly Father.[82]

make **your** day count

Think about the fact that Almighty God created you to have a personal relationship with Him. Then think about the three things God has given you and how they apply to you personally. You are somebody because God created You and lives in You. You are extraordinary!

More Than a History Book

Gloria Copeland

Jesus said, "The words I have spoken to you are spirit and they are life."
—John 6:63

When you meditate on God's Word—that is study it, think about it, and pray about what it says—you're doing more than just reading it. You're taking it into your heart in a very personal way and applying it to your situation.

When you read a Scripture about how God wants you to do well in all areas of life, you won't think, *Hey, that sounds nice, but I'll never become good at any of this academic stuff,* for example. Instead, you'll apply it to yourself and say, "That's right! That's God's Word to me. He says I have the mind of Christ. (1 Cor. 2:16.) He says He'll give me wisdom liberally (James 1:5), and I'm expecting Him to do that for me in this situation I'm facing!"

If you've been reading the Bible like a history book, make a change and begin to see it as God talking directly to you. Take time to meditate on it. Study it. Think about it. Pray about it. Digest it. Take it so personally that it moves from your head to your heart. Then it will become powerful and active in your life![83]

make **your** day count

Ask God to speak to you through His Word, then spend a few minutes reading a chapter of Scripture, perhaps in the book of John or in Psalms. As you read, think of the words as being written especially for you. They were!

time **saving** tips

How to Write a Thank-You Note

Betsy Williams

One of the most thoughtful things you can do is to write prompt thank-you notes to those who have done nice things for you, given you gifts, or invested in your life. It's a way to let the giver know how much you appreciate his or her thoughtfulness and generosity. Thank-you notes needn't be formal or lengthy; yet they should state more than "Thank you for the gift."

Include these elements:

The salutation: "Dear ___________".

Thank the person for the specific thing they did for you or gave you.

If you received a gift, state something brief about how you will use, enjoy, or wear the item.

If you received money, thank the individual for their generosity and state how you might use the money.

You could then state what this person or the gift means to you.

For the closing, you could use the words Sincerely, Love, Bless you, With God's love. There are any number of words you can use. Sincerely is always a safe bet if you are not sure.

easy **recipes**

Oreo® Treats

1 20-oz. bag Oreos, crushed or ground
1 8-oz. cream cheese, softened
20-oz. white almond bark or milk chocolate
Sprinkles (optional)

Mix together Oreos and cream cheese.

Roll into 1-inch balls and place on waxed paper or cookie sheet.

Refrigerate 1 hour.

Melt almond bark or chocolate (in a double boiler is best).

Dip balls into almond bark or chocolate and place on waxed paper or cookie sheet.

Decorate with sprinkles.

Refrigerate until firm.

The Great Exchange

Lindsay Roberts

God took the sinless Christ and poured into him our sins. Then, in exchange, he poured God's goodness into us!

—2 Corinthians 5:21 TLB

Jesus left heaven and came to earth, so we could exchange all the hurts, sadness, sickness, and failures in our lives for everything He was and is.

Philippians 4:19 KJV says, "My God shall supply all your need according to his riches in glory by Christ Jesus." Notice it says "all" your need and "according to *his* riches." God put all the gold and silver in the earth, then told us to take dominion over the earth and subdue it. Next, He gave us "power to get wealth" (Deut. 8:18 KJV). But how many of us are using that power?

A while back I agreed to help my husband, Richard, with a project at Oral Roberts University that turned out to be far more costly than I had anticipated. But when I went to the Lord, saying, "What have I done?" He answered, *It's only money.* He told me that if I would obey the vision He had given me, He would supply the rest. Now when God talks to me about a *program,* I talk to Him about a program, not money.

Would you like to exchange the life you're living for all that Jesus is and has for you? Jesus left the streets of gold so you could have it all. He came to give you everything He is in exchange for everything you are![84]

make **your** day count

Are you dealing with a situation that you would like to exchange for God's goodness, love, and provision? Give that thing to God today and exchange it for His blessing.

Finding a Good Church

Eastman Curtis

Let's see how inventive we can be in encouraging love and helping out, not avoiding worshiping together as some do but spurring each other on, especially as we see the big Day approaching.

—Hebrews 10:25 MESSAGE

A church is a place where you can be encouraged, strengthened, and instructed in the things of God. When you are born again, you are like an infant in many ways. In natural things, we know how dangerous it would be for a little baby to crawl off into the woods and try to raise himself. It isn't possible. The baby just wouldn't survive.

Well, that is exactly what it would be like for you if you didn't find a good church home; you wouldn't survive in your walk with God. So if you and your family don't already attend church together, find a church home for yourself where you can attend regularly and belong—a place where you can get to know the people and they can get to know you.

Visit a few different churches until you find one where you feel like you can grow. If you will stay hungry for God, He will see that you get spiritually fed. He will lead you to the people you need to meet and the places where you need to be.

You should look forward to going to church because it's one of your best opportunities to learn more about God. Church can be an exciting place to be as you sense the work of the Holy Spirit in your life.[85]

make **your** day count

If you don't already have a church home where you can grow spiritually and hang out with Christian friends, seek out a strong believer and ask about his or her church. You could also call a Christian radio station for leads. Make plans to visit the church's next service. Take a friend with you!

Memorizing God's Word

Sarah Bowling

Jesus said, "The Counselor, the Holy Spirit, whom the Father will send in my name, will teach you all things and will remind you of everything I have said to you."
—John 14:26

Meditating on God's Word is essential if it is going to become part of your life, and the first step is to memorize it. But don't let the word *memorize* make you nervous. Jesus said in the verse above that He has instructed the Holy Spirit to help us.

One of my friends started memorizing Scripture when she was first saved. Since she knew nothing about the Bible or Christianity, her mind was a blank slate on which God could write who He is and what He does. It cleansed her mind from the past and centered it on what God says, what it means to be saved, and who we are in Christ.

Another friend told me about her son who had been diagnosed with Attention Deficit Disorder (ADD) and was having some rather serious difficulties with his behavior and grades. His mom and he agreed that he should try memorizing some of the Bible, so he began working on the book of Proverbs a little bit at a time. By the end of that semester, his grades had gone up from very low C's to low A's and high B's.

Both the mother and the son attributed this improvement to his memorizing the book of Proverbs.

God's Word will change your life. Begin memorizing some of it today![86]

make **your** day count

Use the tips on the next page to begin memorizing two or three of your favorite Bible passages.

time **saving** tips

Memorizing God's Word[87]

Sarah Bowling

Write the verses on "stickies" and put them in places where you'll see them often (the bathroom mirror, in your car, on your computer monitor, etc.).

Practice reciting the verses to the rhythm of your walking or exercising.

Write the verses on cards and keep them in the restroom, so you can look at them when you're "resting."

Review the verses at lunch and on breaks.

First thing in the morning, read the verses out loud several times.

Write the verses out several times.

Begin memorizing a new verse the last thing before going to bed each night.

easy **recipes**

Bird's Nest Treats

¼ cup butter or margarine
4½ cups mini marshmallows
¼ cup creamy peanut butter
¼ cup semisweet chocolate chips
4 cups chow mein noodles
1 cup jelly beans or candy eggs

In large saucepan over medium heat, melt butter and marshmallows.

Add peanut butter and chocolate chips. Stir for 2 minutes or until smooth.

Remove from heat. Stir in chow mein noodles.

Divide into 12 mounds on wax paper.

Use fingers to shape into nests when cool enough to handle.

Finish by putting 3 or 4 "eggs" into each nest.

Experience God's Love for Yourself

Suzanne Rentz

[That you may really come] to know [practically, through experience for yourselves] the love of Christ, which far surpasses mere knowledge [without experience].

—Ephesians 3:19 AMP

I speak well of my husband—my sons' father—but I don't make him out to be some incredible superhero. Yet they know that he's strong and big and smart, because they have experienced his strength and his wisdom for themselves.

He sometimes wrestles with them, and at bedtime he often carries all of them upstairs at the same time. When they go through a tough time, he has good advice for them. He's got a hug and a kiss for them every night. He spends time with them. So they not only know their dad, but they've experienced an intimate, father-son relationship with him; they know how much he loves them.

Do you know that God, our heavenly Father, longs for us to know Him and how much He loves us? If we can ever really grasp the truth about who our Father is and the depth of His love for us, I believe that it will be the bridge that connects us to God, that takes head knowledge (knowing about God) and applies it to the heart (knowing Him intimately).

Don't settle for only knowing *about* God. Spend time with Him in prayer and through His Word. Get to know Him and His love for you—on a personal basis. Once you experience God for yourself, you'll never settle for less.[88]

make **your** day count

How well do you know God? Do you know what others say about Him? Do you know what the Bible says about Him? Real fulfillment comes from knowing God for yourself, on a personal basis. Tell God today that you really want to know Him. Make it your great quest.

God Loves Us All

Blaine Bartel

Your Master also is in heaven; neither is there respect of persons with him.
—Ephesians 6:9 KJV

One of America's greatest leaders brought needed change to this country as he spoke these words: "I have a dream that my four little children will one day live in a nation where they will not be judged by the color of their skin but by the content of their character." Dr. Martin Luther King Jr. saw that it was unbiblical for people to respect one person over another because of skin color.

Unfortunately, we live in a world where some people do judge others for their skin color, financial status, or social background. Fortunately for us, God does not. He looks at our hearts, not what's on the outside. God isn't a respecter of persons; He doesn't love you less or more than He loves anyone else.

Some people feel they have to earn God's love, but He can't love you any more than He does right now, because He loves you with all His heart. God may be more pleased with your decisions and actions than another person's, but that doesn't mean God loves them less and you more. People will reap the rewards of the decision to serve or reject God, but that doesn't change God's love for them. God loves the sinner and the saint, the rich and the poor. God is just and fair; He loves us all the same.[89]

make **your** day count

Think about how it makes you feel to know that God loves you just as much as He loves Jesus or any other person who has ever lived. Keep this in mind as you go through your day and encounter others. Love them all the same, just like God does.

God's Not Mad at You

Kenneth Copeland

You are merciful and gentle, Lord, slow in getting angry, full of constant lovingkindness and of truth.

—Psalm 86:15 TLB

I have six simple words for you: God is not mad at you!

The first time I found that out, I hadn't been a Christian very long. I had heard all my life about the terrible things God would do to you. He would make you sick and keep you poor. He would bring you trouble to make you strong. I heard He did bad things to you, but it was all right because He was God.

Then one day I came across Isaiah 54. God is not mad at us! That's earthshaking news—such good news that some people have a hard time believing it. They start thinking of all the sin they've allowed into their lives, all the wrongs they've done.

But God did something about that: He sent Jesus to the cross.

Read Isaiah 52. All of us have seen paintings of the Crucifixion. Yet none of them come close to the horror of what happened to Jesus that day. When He bore the sins of mankind, His body became so marred, He didn't even look human. (v. 14.)

Yet it was this very event that freed us forever from God's wrath. Jesus' death on the cross was enough to pay for your sins and mine. As far as God is concerned, it's all over. We just have to accept it.[90]

make **your** day count

Study Isaiah 52, 53, and 54. Let this eye-opening news sink in and change the way you think. God isn't mad at you! He loves you! Just the way you are, right where you are!

Overcoming Eating Disorders: Replacing Lies with Truth

Nancy Alcorn

Jesus said, "You will know the truth, and the truth will set you free."

—John 8:32

One of the major steps in overcoming eating disorders is to identify the lies we believe about ourselves so that they can be replaced by the truth of God's Word. This is a process, however, and it takes time.

When you start to feel depressed or have the urge to binge, purge, or engage in self-destructive behavior, start to write down the thoughts you are having at the time. It may sound something like this: *I am so fat and ugly. If I binge and purge, I will feel better. I must be crazy!*

These are lies and accusations about yourself that must be changed into positive thoughts! After you write down these thoughts, search God's Word for the truth. It is not enough to simply not think these negative thoughts. You must aggressively replace the negative thoughts with God's truth.

Some paraphrased Scriptures that would replace the lies mentioned above are: "I am beautifully and wonderfully made. I will cry out to the Lord with my pain and He will set me free. God has not given me a spirit of fear, but of power, love, and a sound mind. God loves me and accepts me, just as I am."[91]

If you or someone you know is struggling with an eating disorder, there is hope, help, and healing through God and His Word.[92]

make **your** day count

Even if you don't have an eating disorder, believing lies about yourself will only bring you down. Write down your negative thoughts today, then find Scriptures to replace them.

time **saving** tips

Eating Disorder Warning Signs[93]

Nancy Alcorn

When people think of "eating disorders," they often think of an extremely thin, emaciated person. However, binge eating is also considered an eating disorder and has similar root issues and causes as anorexia and bulimia. These are some characteristics of people with an eating disorder.

Feeling fat and ugly, then turning to diet pills, laxatives, and diuretics to control weight gain.

The person "disappears" to the bathroom as soon as he or she finishes meals. This is consistent with the purging seen in bulimia nervosa.

Individual is always cold, even in warm weather. Wears things like baggy sweatshirts or sweaters, long pants, and always has on socks. Clothes don't seem to fit; always look baggy.

Individual hides food rather than eating it. Hides food in things like pockets and napkins; indicative of anorexia nervosa.

With bulimia nervosa, individual purges in bathrooms, paper bags, closets, pockets, jars, etc.

Excessive exercise to burn calories. Individual often hides exercise habit out of shame.

Significant weight gain. Individual eats large amounts of food, often more quickly than others, takes unusually large bites of food, and grazes throughout the day. Normally interactive with others, but begins to withdraw.

easy **recipes**

Everyone's Favorite Green Bean Casserole

Betsy Williams

2 16-oz. bags frozen French cut green beans
1 can cream of mushroom soup
1 can Durkee or French's onion rings
Salt and pepper

Cook green beans according to package directions.

In a medium-size bowl, mix together green beans and soup.

Salt and pepper to taste.

Put in a greased 9 x 13 inch casserole dish.

Bake at 350° for 30 minutes or until bubbly.

For last 10 minutes, top with onion rings.

Passing the Stress Test

Lindsay Roberts

Count it all joy when you fall into various trials, knowing that the testing of your faith produces patience. But let patience have its perfect work, that you may be perfect and complete, lacking nothing. If any of you lacks wisdom, let him ask of God…and it will be given to him.

—James 1:2–5 NKJV

Are you under enormous pressure? God has not called you to be stressed, frustrated, or upset. Let's look at what the Word of God says about what you can do to take control of stress and pass the stress test.

First, count it all joy. You do it because you know this: that the trying of your faith works patience, and when patience has had its perfect work, you will be left wanting nothing! I believe that when we count it all joy, it causes God to come on the scene and Satan to go the other direction.

Second, remember that God is working in you. Let patience have her perfect work. Most people think patience is waiting and doing nothing until something happens. Not true! *Patience* means hopeful endurance, tolerance, diligence, self-possessed waiting, and dogged tenacity.

Third, ask for wisdom. Notice that we do the asking and God does the answering.

There are many great Scriptures to help you deal with stress, but until you apply them, they might as well be fairy dust to you. It's time to decide, "I will not react to stress and fall apart, but I will respond with the Word of God!" Choosing the right attitude in the middle of stress can bring the answers from the Lord.[94]

make **your** day count

In whatever stressful situation you find yourself today, declare, "I will not let stress overtake me. According to God's Word, I count it all joy, and I will patiently endure so that I will lack nothing!"

Hungry for God

Eastman Curtis

Now glory be to God who by his mighty power at work within us is able to do far more than we would ever dare to ask or even dream of—infinitely beyond our highest prayers, desires, thoughts, or hopes.

—Ephesians 3:20 TLB

If you think the Christian life is boring, it is probably because your spirit has become satisfied with the status quo instead of staying hungry for God. When you are satisfied, you become spiritually stagnant. And if you have ever seen or smelled a stagnant pond, you know what I mean when I say stagnant. It's not a pretty—or a sweet-smelling—picture!

When you are hungry for more of God, He will begin to change you and you won't be able to stay the same for long. As a matter of fact, following God and the leading of His Spirit will often lead to a life of high adventure that you never could have expected or imagined.

Unfortunately, some people confuse religion with God. But the two are definitely not the same. Religion is man-inspired and often lacks the approval and infusion of the Spirit of God. On the other hand, when God gets involved with man, there is a relationship that is dynamic, not static.

That kind of dynamic relationship with God doesn't just happen in church, because He goes with you wherever you go. With God, anything can happen if you are open to His leading and you are listening to Him as you go.

So get hungry for a relationship with God. Then hold on to your hat—because life will be anything but boring![95]

make **your** day count

Ask God to create a hunger in you for Him, His Word, and His Spirit. As you begin to give attention to the things of God, that hunger and desire will increase. Spend some time with Him today.

Knockout

Blaine Bartel

We are pressed on every side by troubles, but not crushed and broken. We are perplexed because we don't know why things happen as they do, but we don't give up and quit.
—2 Corinthians 4:8 TLB

An unusual fight happened in the early 1900s. A boxer known as C.D. was furiously swinging at his opponent without much success. Fed up with his opponent's ability to avoid his punches, C.D. put all his might into one single punch, hoping that it would knock his challenger's lights out. He swung so hard that when his opponent moved to avoid the punch, C.D. wasn't able to stop the momentum of his swing. His punch came all the way around and landed right in his own face, knocking him out. The referee gave the ten count, and C.D. lost the fight.

It sounds weird to us that someone could lose by knocking himself out, but it happens all the time—maybe not in a boxing match, but in the arena of the great game called life. We are in a fight called the "fight of faith." The fight has been fixed for us by Jesus' dying on the cross for our sins.

But even though we can't lose in life, many people still do. They either get knocked down by a circumstance, trial, or bad decision of their own and refuse to get back up; or they simply quit the fight and forfeit. You can't lose unless you quit or don't get back up. Don't knock yourself out in a fight you have already won.[96]

make **your** day count

Have you been beating yourself up with negative thoughts? Do you want to quit? If so, instead of focusing your attention on yourself, set your thoughts instead on the great triumph Jesus won for you when He was raised from the dead. Get Him involved. He'll help you win!

time **saving** tips

Things You Can Do to Help Grow Your Church Family[97]

Sarah Bowling

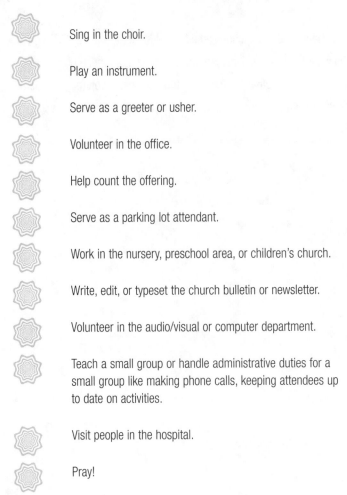

- Sing in the choir.
- Play an instrument.
- Serve as a greeter or usher.
- Volunteer in the office.
- Help count the offering.
- Serve as a parking lot attendant.
- Work in the nursery, preschool area, or children's church.
- Write, edit, or typeset the church bulletin or newsletter.
- Volunteer in the audio/visual or computer department.
- Teach a small group or handle administrative duties for a small group like making phone calls, keeping attendees up to date on activities.
- Visit people in the hospital.
- Pray!

easy **recipes**

Fruit Pizza

1 roll refrigerated sugar cookie dough
1 cup sugar
1 8-oz. cream cheese, softened
1 8-oz. Cool Whip
1 small can crushed pineapple
1 or 2 kiwi, peeled and cut into thin slices
Fresh strawberries, cleaned, hulled, and thinly sliced
Bananas, sliced and dipped in lemon juice (to prevent browning)
Shredded coconut
Finely chopped pecans

Spread sugar cookie dough evenly on a pizza pan using fingertips.

Pierce a few times with fork tines and bake at temperature listed on package until lightly browned.

If it puffs up, press down slightly after you let it cool a little. Cool crust completely.

Beat softened cream cheese with sugar until smooth.

Fold in Cool Whip and blend thoroughly.

Spread this on the cooled crust.

Drain pineapple thoroughly and spread evenly over cream cheese mixture.

Arrange the slices of kiwi on top of the pineapple, then arrange the strawberry and banana slices.

Sprinkle with shredded coconut and chopped pecans.

Refrigerate until serving. Cut into pizza slices to serve.

Check Your Affections

Gloria Copeland

Run in such a way as to get the prize. Everyone who competes in the games goes into strict training. They do it to get a crown that will not last; but we do it to get a crown that will last forever.

—1 Corinthians 9:24,25

Separating yourself from the ways of the world doesn't always mean just leaving bad habits behind. It often means simply getting rid of those things that don't build you up.

Hebrews 12:1 says that as we run the race that is set before us, we are to throw off everything that hinders us. You may have things in your life that are slowing you down spiritually. They may not be bad things in themselves, yet they are draining you. You may be so wrapped up in your computer, for instance, that you spend all your time thinking and talking about it. Or you may have joined a club or taken up a hobby that has become the center of your attention.

The problem with things like that is not that they are sinful; it's that they've captured your affection. It's time to check your affections. The Bible says in Colossians 3 that we're to set our affection on things above, not on things on the earth.

God wants you to set the affection of your heart on Him. Why? So that He can pour out His affection on you!

You can't give anything to God without His giving you more in return. When you set your affection on Him, He will give you more than you can imagine![98]

make **your** day count

Are there things—even good things—that have captured your affections to the point that they are hindering your walk with God? If so, strip off those weights, lighten your load, and build yourself up by spending time with God. Run your race well. Run to win!

Personalization of God's Word

Sarah Bowling

All Scripture is God-breathed and is useful for teaching, rebuking, correcting and training in righteousness.

—2 Timothy 3:16

An important part of meditating on God's Word is personalization. Personalizing the verses you meditate on is an invaluable tool. Think about how the Scripture applies to your life. How does it change you, comfort you, or challenge you? Make it personal; apply it to yourself and your situations.

One of my friends once confided he was having a very difficult time memorizing but had overcome his frustration by picturing himself in the verses being memorized. Not only can you put yourself into the events that are being described or discussed in the verses, you can also replace *I, me, my,* etc. with your name.

For example, if I were meditating on 2 Corinthians 5:17 KJV, I would read it like this: "If [Sarah] be in Christ, [Sarah] is a new creature: old things are passed away; behold, all things are become new."

As we personalize God's Word, it becomes alive and active in our hearts. Personalizing it helps us to see its relevance in our lives. Then the Word is able to change us and shape us into God's image as we yield to it. Ask the Holy

Spirit to make the Word you are memorizing personal and applicable to you. Put yourself in the verses, savoring them as descriptions of who you are.[99]

make **your** day count

Find a couple of verses of Scripture that apply to a situation you are dealing with. Then personalize them by putting your name in them.

Finding the Perfect Job

Eastman Curtis

Trust in the Lord with all your heart
and lean not on your own understanding;
in all your ways acknowledge him,
and he will make your paths straight.

—Proverbs 3:5,6

First of all, there is no perfect job. What you want isn't "the perfect job," but the job that will best fit your ability, interests, and personality. And there's great news: God has already chosen a career for you!

Ask God to help you make the day-by-day decisions that will eventually get you where you need to be. Then listen to the Holy Spirit and follow through on whatever He nudges you to do that day. In the meantime, be faithful right where you are, because God will probably use where you are to prepare you for where you are going.

Let's say you feel that God has given you the desire to become an engineer. Try to get a job at your level in that field, even if it means becoming an errand boy. As you work at that job, you will start to find out whether or not you really fit in the engineering field.

If engineering seems to fit, find out what is required to qualify for the job, then start doing your part right now—

prepare your résumé, fill out job applications, and contact key people.

After you have done all you can do, let God do the rest. He knows what needs to happen to make your desire a reality, and He will take care of the rest.[100]

make **your** day count

What field do you believe God has chosen for you? If you're not sure, think about the things you enjoy doing the most and determine if they fit into any particular professions. Do at least one thing today toward establishing yourself in one of those professions.

time **saving** tips

Six Keys to Being Promoted by Your Boss[101]

Blaine Bartel

Here are six keys to your promotion at your work:

Always arrive a few minutes early for work and then stay at least a few minutes late.

Do not allow personal issues or other relationships at your job to take time or focus away from your work.

Never complain about your pay. You agreed to work for that amount, so be grateful!

Ask your boss from time to time if there is anything you can do to improve your performance.

Work with your head, not just your hands. Think of ways to do your job more effectively.

Don't continually badger your boss with requests for promotions or raises. Let your work do the talking, pray, and trust God; and when the timing is right, ask to speak to your boss, without being demanding.

Super Spud

Betsy Williams

Baked potato
Cottage cheese
Cheddar cheese, grated
Tomato, chopped
Green onions chopped
Black olives, sliced or chopped
Salt and pepper
Any other toppings that appeal to you

Bake potato by method you like best.

After it is baked, use a knife to cut the potato open lengthwise, but do not cut in two. Lay open the potato so that insides are face up, and slightly mash. (Leave skins on for optimum nutrition.)

Spread a layer of cottage cheese over the potato, then a layer of cheese.

Continue layering other ingredients according to your taste.

Voilà! Dinner is served.

Healing for the Wounded Heart

Nancy Alcorn

The Spirit of the Lord God is upon me; because the Lord hath anointed me to preach good tidings unto the meek; he hath sent me to bind up the brokenhearted, to proclaim liberty to the captives, and the opening of the prison to them that are bound.

—Isaiah 61:1 KJV

Jesus came to heal broken hearts. When we have been wounded and hurt by others, it is important that we forgive and let go of all bitterness. Matthew 6:14 tells us that if we will not forgive others, then God cannot forgive us. If we choose to forgive as an act of our will, out of obedience to God, we can experience God's forgiveness and then ask for healing in those areas where we have been wounded.

By allowing the Holy Spirit to bring to your mind past hurts, you can ask Him to show you the truth of the situation. Many times the Holy Spirit may show you that it was not your fault, that you were not to blame. God may reveal during this prayer time that He was protecting you from even greater harm. In whatever ways He chooses to do it, God can bring you peace and restoration from your hurts and wounds if you invite Him into your circumstances.

God is calling you—He wants you to know that He cares and is willing to meet you right where you are, right in the middle of your mess. He is knocking at the door of your heart right now. Why don't you answer? Your future depends on it![102]

make **your** day count

Have you experienced hurts and wounds that have hindered you in any way? Take the situations and individuals that are responsible to God in prayer. As an act of your will, choose to forgive the offenders.

The Divorce Filter

Suzanne Rentz

I am the Lord, I change not.

—Malachi 3:6 KJV

Life experiences can create a filter that distorts how we see God. Divorce is one of them. In the beginning, your life may be rolling along, smooth, steady, secure in the solid foundation of your family. Then all of a sudden your life is turned upside down because your parents are divorcing. Now everything you thought was up is down. Your security has crumbled.

A friend of mine whose parents divorced shared, "I felt this incredible, deep sadness. There were times when I felt like it was my fault, maybe if I hadn't been born, maybe I was just in the way." She had nothing to do with the divorce, yet this is a common feeling among children from divorced families.

As children, we take in what's happening and apply it to our lives and often get confused. Only recently has my friend come to the place where she's feeling stronger and more secure.

If you experience divorce, it can become a filter that causes you to wonder, *God, are You upside down just like the rest of my world? My family life and everything I knew has crumbled. Have You left me too?*

If that describes how you feel, remember that your life may change, but Jesus never changes. (Heb. 13:8.) He said, "I will never leave you nor forsake you" (Heb. 13:5 NKJV).[103]

make **your** day count

If you've experienced your parents' divorce or some other negative circumstance that has distorted your view of God, talk to God about it. Ask Him to help you see any faulty thinking you've come to believe. Go to His Word for the truth and choose to believe it by faith.

Get Bitter or Get Better

Lindsay Roberts

Watch out that no bitterness takes root among you,
for as it springs up it causes deep trouble,
hurting many in their spiritual lives.

—Hebrews 12:15 TLB

Throughout my miscarriages and losing my precious son after just thirty-six hours, I repeatedly had to choose whether I was going to get *bitter and be destroyed* or get *better and let God take over.* It was a decision that only I could make, and I knew that once I made the choice, there would be no turning back. If I was going to get better, I had to believe in what I was doing and never let go. Otherwise, I knew that the grief, anxiety, and hurt would eat me alive.

In your trials you, too, must recognize the fine line between getting bitter and getting better and decide which way you are going to go. This is not an area in which you can "straddle the fence" or change sides. Bitterness will tear you up and do permanent damage unless you make the choice to grab it and take control of it.

At one point, it hit me like a ton of bricks that God was my God no matter what happened, not just if He healed me or my children. I had to follow Isaiah 43:18,19: "Forget the former things; do not dwell on the past. See, I am doing a new thing!"

It is not easy, but once you decide not to get bitter, it will be your day of new beginnings as it was for me.[104]

make **your** day count

Are you harboring bitterness inside about a wrong that has been done to you, a disappointment you have faced? God is still God and He wants to give you a new beginning. Give Him that bitterness today, and then get ready for the good things He will do.

time **saving** tips

Five Roads to Popularity Without Losing Your Reputation[105]

Blaine Bartel

Everyone wants to be popular. Popularity isn't a bad thing. In fact, Jesus was very popular during much of His ministry. He never compromised His character or morals to gain acceptance, however. Here are five roads to popularity while maintaining your integrity.

Be a kind person. You will never be short on friends.

When you do something, do it with all your might. Excellence draws a crowd.

Promote others and their accomplishments, not your own. God will then be able to exalt you.

Dare to dream big and pray for the seemingly impossible. People are drawn to those filled with hope and faith.

Stand up for what is right. Our world today is desperately searching for real heroes.

easy **recipes**

Mini Pizzas

Betsy Williams

English muffins, split in two
Jar of spaghetti sauce
Sliced pepperoni
Mozzarella cheese, grated
Any other pizza toppings you like

Place muffin halves face up.

Spread spaghetti sauce on them.

Place a couple of pepperoni slices and any other toppings on top of sauce.

Sprinkle cheese on top.

Put "pizzas" on broiler pan of toaster oven (not on rack), and then place in toaster oven. (You can use traditional oven.)

Broil until muffins brown on the edges and cheese melts.

Visualization of God's Word

Sarah Bowling

Open my eyes that I may see
wonderful things in your law.
—Psalm 119:18

Visualization is a key element of meditating on God's Word. God often uses word pictures to illustrate spiritual principles. When we visualize those word pictures, God's Word comes alive for us. The book of Proverbs is full of word pictures. For example, in Proverbs 1, wisdom is pictured as a woman calling out in the streets for someone who will value her words. Jesus taught by using nature to visually portray the kingdom of heaven. In Matthew 5:13–16, Jesus describes believers as "the salt of the earth" and "the light of the world."

We tend to remember things better when we see them or when we use our imagination to create vivid situations and pictures in which we are personally involved, but not all Scriptures lend themselves so readily to visualization. Sometimes you have to be a little more creative and use your imagination.

For example, if I were meditating on 1 John 1:9—"If we confess our sins, he is faithful and just and will forgive us our sins and purify us from all unrighteousness,"—I would picture Jesus telling me from the cross that He has forgiven me. Then, I would picture myself writing my sins on a giant chalkboard. Jesus would walk up with a garden hose and wash them all away.

Visualizing God's Word will revolutionize your life.[106]

make **your** day count

Read the Scripture passages mentioned in the devotion above and visualize yourself in them.

Be a Person of Influence

Eastman Curtis

Make the most of your chances to tell others the Good News. Be wise in all your contacts with them. Let your conversation be gracious as well as sensible, for then you will have the right answer for everyone.

—Colossians 4:5-6 TLB

God wants you to make a difference in your high school. If you really want to do that, follow these five suggestions. I guarantee that if you will do them, you will make a significant impact for Jesus.

1. Wear a Christian T-shirt so that everywhere you go, you will be preaching a message about Jesus.
2. Carry your Bible to every class, and read it when you have some extra time.
3. Pray over your lunch, not only because it needs to be prayed over, but because it will remind those around you of God's presence, even in the lunchroom.
4. Read one chapter of the Bible each day in the cafeteria.
5. Answer the questions people ask about Jesus—and I promise you, they will ask. When they do, be sure to brag on Him!

If you are walking boldly with the Lord, you are like a fruit tree as you bear the fruit of the Spirit. (Gal. 5:22,23.) When others see your fruit, they will know that you are different from those in the world.

Sometimes you have to step out of your comfort zone and be a vessel of God's love to those who aren't saved yet. If you will do this, you will make a difference for God in this world.[107]

make **your** day count

Pick one of these five suggestions and put one into practice today. People will notice you, so be sure you conduct yourself in a way that will honor God. Your life may be the only Bible some people ever see.

You Are That Temple

Gloria Copeland

If anyone destroys God's temple, God will destroy him;
for God's temple is sacred, and you are that temple.
—1 Corinthians 3:17

If you've made Jesus your Lord, God has called you to be holy. That's your destiny. That's where you're headed. Romans 8:29 says that God "predestined [us] to be conformed to the likeness of his Son."

As a Christian, you have been made holy. Now you are called to live on the outside what you are on the inside. To be like Jesus, you have to give yourself completely to Him. That's how you're changed to be like Him.

Becoming more like Him—living like Jesus would—is a process. Your spirit has been completely changed, but your soul—your mind, will, and emotions—and your body are changed to be more like Him over time.

You are on a journey. The Bible says you are changed by the Holy Spirit to be more like Him, as you look at Him in the Word. (2 Cor. 3:18 AMP.)

Many people become Christians, but they never disconnect from their old lives. They never spend enough time reading the Bible, praying, or listening to the Holy Spirit within them, allowing Him to teach them how to separate from the world. As a result, they never change on the outside.

Your freedom comes when you change on the outside. That's when you experience all that God has provided for you. That's when you'll walk in holiness.[108]

make **your** day count

What is one way you can disconnect from your old life today? Take that step and put God's Word in its place. Look up 2 Corinthians 5:17 and think about what that verse means to your new life in Christ.

The Eye of Faith

Blaine Bartel

Faith is being sure of what we hope for and certain of what we do not see.

—Hebrews 11:1

At the end of the 1800s, Bishop Milton Wright used to travel to colleges and speak about the soon second coming of Christ. One evening, while eating supper at a college president's house, Bishop Wright was asked by his host why he was so sure Christ was returning at any moment. He responded, "My good sir, everything that man can accomplish He has already done."

The president of the college politely said, "I respect your opinion, but I disagree. Man hasn't flown yet."

Bishop Wright firmly responded, "If God intended man to fly, He would have made him like the angels and created him with wings."

Bishop Wright limited his ability to believe by what he could see. However, he had two sons who could believe in something before they could see it—Orville and Wilbur Wright who built and flew the first airplane.

Some people can't believe it if they can't see it, taste it, or touch it. But God asks us to live by faith. We can't always see His promises to us, but we are asked to take Him at His

Word. When He said, "By [Jesus'] stripes you were healed" (1 Peter 2:24 NKJV), He asked us to believe we are healed even though we may not feel healed. Before we ever see it, we must first believe it. Then we will receive it.[109]

make **your** day count

Find a Bible promise for the thing you need most. God asks us to believe His promises are true, even before we see them come to pass. Choose today to take God at His Word, even if it looks impossible. He honors His Word, and He won't let you down.

A Blueprint That Works

Lindsay Roberts

Be doers of the word, and not hearers only.

—James 1:22 NKJV

In math we learn that two plus two equals four. And every time we add those numbers, the result is the same. However, if we change the *plus* to a *minus,* we destroy the equation and the answer becomes quite different.

God has given us a plan and a purpose—plus a specific procedure to fulfill that plan. It's called the Word of God. As we pour ourselves into Scripture, we soon begin to understand that God's blueprint will work again and again.

There are two reasons we can trust what our heavenly Father declares:

1. God's Word is truth. "God is not a man, that he should lie" (Num. 23:19 KJV).
2. God's Word never changes. God declares, "I am the Lord, I change not" (Mal. 3:6 KJV).

You were not created to be perpetually stressed, frustrated, and upset. That is not God's desire. He sees you winning in life. Deuteronomy 28:13 says, "The Lord will make you the head, not the tail. If you pay attention to the commands of the Lord your God that I give you this day and carefully follow them, you will always be at the top, never at the bottom."

It's a lot like having a drawer full of makeup. What a difference it makes when you actually apply it. God's Word is just the same.[110]

make **your** day count

Instead of being overtaken by stress, find a Scripture on God's peace and meditate on it today. For example, you could ponder Philippians 4:6–7 and pray, "Thank You, God, for Your peace that passes my understanding. Help me walk in Your peace, so I won't worry today."

About the Author

Lindsay Roberts and her husband, Richard, were married in 1980. She began traveling with her husband, ministering throughout the world and supporting him in what the Lord has called him to do.

"After the birth of our son, Richard Oral," Lindsay says, "we were devastated when he lived only 36 hours. But God picked us up, dried our tears, and helped us try again." Out of that experience from pain to victory, Lindsay wrote *36 Hours with an Angel*—the story of how God sustained their faith after Richard Oral's death and blessed her and Richard with the miracle births of their three daughters: Jordan, Olivia, and Chloe.

Lindsay hosts *Make Your Day Count,* a daily television program full of ministry, cooking, creative tips, and lots of fun. With her husband, Richard, she also co-hosts the nightly television program, *The Hour of Healing.*

She has co-authored several books, such as *A Cry for Miracles* and *Dear God, I Love To Eat, But I Sure Do Hate To Cook* cookbook. She has also written several children's books, including *ABC's of Faith for Children* and *God's Champions.*

Lindsay serves as editor of *Make Your Day Count,* a quarterly magazine aimed at today's woman; *Miracles Now,* a quarterly magazine for ministry partners; and *Your Daily Guide to Miracles,* a daily devotional book published semi-annually.

She is also a member of the Oral Roberts University Board of Regents.

"I am dedicated to God and willing to do whatever He calls me to do," Lindsay says. "I also stand in support of the call of God upon my husband. He and I are both grateful that God is using us for His glory."

Royalties from the sale of this book and others
in the *Make Your Day Count* series will go towards
the Make Your Day Count Scholarship Fund.

To contact Lindsay Roberts
or request a free issue of the
Make Your Day Count magazine,
please write to:

Lindsay Roberts
c/o Oral Roberts Ministries
Tulsa, Oklahoma 74171-0001
or
e-mail her at:
Lindsay@orm.cc

Please visit the *Make Your Day Count* Web site at
www.makeyourdaycount.com.

*Please include your prayer requests
and comments when you write.*

If you would like to have someone join in agreement with you in prayer as a point of contact, consider calling the Abundant Life Prayer Group at 918-495-7777. They are there to pray with you twenty-four hours a day, seven days a week.

About the Contributors

Nancy Alcorn is president and founder of Mercy Ministries of America, a residential facility for troubled girls ages 13-28. Presently, Mercy Ministries operates homes and licensed adoption agencies in various cities around the world. Plans are underway to open additional homes in the United States and in other countries. To contact Mercy Ministries, call (615) 831-6987 or visit www.mercyministries.com.

Dr. Patricia D. Bailey is a lecturer, author, and founder of Master's Touch Ministries International, a mission outreach. M.T.M. has also founded Y.U.G.O. (Young Adults United for Global Outreach) and Sister to Sister, an international outreach to women in foreign countries. Dr. Bailey serves as a missions strategy consultant to several growing churches and has developed leadership programs around the world. Master's Touch Ministries has headquarters in Atlanta; Los Angeles; and London, England. Dr. Bailey is the proud mother of a son, Karim Israel Bailey. To contact Patricia, call (770) 521-0318 or visit www.mtmintl.org.

Blaine Bartel is one of America's premiere leadership specialists. Blaine served as Oneighty®'s youth pastor for 7 years, helping it become America's largest local church youth ministry, reaching more than 2,500 students each week. He is now the National Director of Oneighty® and Associate Pastor of 12,000-member Church On The Move in Tulsa, Oklahoma. Blaine has served under his pastor and mentor, Willie George, for more than 20 years. God has uniquely gifted him to teach local church staff and workers to thrive while faithfully serving the vision of their leader. Known for his creativity and respected for his achievements, Blaine uses Thrive audio resource to equip thousands of church and youth leaders each month with principles, ideas, and strategies that work. To contact Blaine, write Blaine Bartel, Serving America's Future, P.O. Box 691923, Tulsa, Oklahoma 74169, or visit www.blainebartel.com.

Sarah Bowling is the daughter of Pastor Wallace and Marilyn Hickey. Her God-given gifts for Bible teaching and ministry are enthusiastically received by television audiences and churches throughout the world. Currently, Sarah is ministering "Jump-Start Your Heart" clinics to church congregations around the country, which are designed to breathe new life into the believer's walk with God and to help believers regain their edge spiritually, emotionally, and mentally. Sarah and her husband, Reece, live in Denver, Colorado, where they are on staff at Marilyn Hickey Ministries/Orchard Road Christian Center. To contact Sarah, write Marilyn Hickey Ministries, P.O. Box 17340, Denver, Colorado 80217, or visit www.mhmin.org.

Kenneth and Gloria Copeland are the bestselling authors of more than 60 books such as the popular *Walk with God, Managing God's Mutual Funds,* and *God's Will for You.* Together they have co-authored numerous other books, including *Family Promises* and *Load Up Devotional for Teens.* As founders of Kenneth Copeland Ministries in Fort Worth, Texas, Kenneth and Gloria are in their 33rd year of circling the globe with the uncompromised Word of God, preaching and teaching a lifestyle of victory for every Christian.

Their daily and Sunday *Believer's Voice of Victory* television broadcasts now air on more than 500 stations around the world, and their *Believer's Voice of Victory* and *Shout!* magazines are distributed to more than 1 million adults and children worldwide. To learn more about Kenneth Copeland Ministries you may visit our Web site at www.kcm.org or call 1-800-600-7395.

Marty Copeland is a certified personal trainer, fitness instructor, and nutritional guidance counselor. She is a wife and mother of three children. For more information on **weight loss** and **fitness products** you may contact Marty at www.martycopeland.com or by calling (800) 600-7395.

Eastman Curtis is the senior pastor of one of the fastest growing churches in America, Destiny Church. He is also the host of two award-winning television programs, *This Generation* and *Destiny TV,* as well as the creator and distributor of *This Generation* radio devotionals. Eastman offers an internship program for young adults ages eighteen to twenty-five who devote an entire year of their lives to the ministry. During this year of hands-on training, each intern is given the opportunity to gain valuable administrative experience and travel the United States hosting meetings at churches and schools. Eastman and his wife, Angel, reside in Tulsa, Oklahoma with their two children, Sumner and Nicole. To contact Eastman, call (800) 5ON-FIRE (566-3473) or visit www.destinychurch.com.

Kim Freeman is a writer, researcher, and Bible teacher, whose practical, no-nonsense approach to the Word of God makes it both easy to understand and apply. Born and raised in St. Louis, Missouri, Kim holds a bachelor of arts degree in psychology from the University of Missouri and currently serves as part of the management team at Church On The Rock in St. Peters, Missouri. To contact Kim, call (636) 240-7775 or email her at kfreeman@cotr.org.

Kellie Copeland Kutz is a speaker, author, musician, wife, and mother of four. She directs the development of all Kenneth Copeland Ministries' children's products and is the contributing editor for *Shout! The Voice of Victory for Kids,* a monthly children's magazine. She is best known as Commander Kellie—the fearless, faith-filled adventurer in the *Commander Kellie and the SuperKids*SM videos, audio series, and novels. To contact Kellie, visit www.kcm.org or call (800) 600-7395.

Kate McVeigh is known as a solid evangelist and teacher of the Gospel, with a powerful anointing to heal the sick and win the lost. A graduate of Rhema Bible Training Center in Tulsa, Oklahoma, her outreach includes books, teaching tapes, a daily radio broadcast, and a weekly television broadcast. Kate's down-to-earth and often humorous teaching of the Word motivates many to attain God's best for their lives. To contact Kate, call (586) 795-8885 or visit www.katemcveigh.org.

Terri Copeland Pearsons and her husband, George, are pastors of Eagle Mountain International Church. The eldest daughter of Kenneth Copeland, Terri leads the prayer life at EMIC. She also ministers and travels on behalf of her father for Kenneth Copeland Ministries and her husband, George, for Eagle Mountain International Church throughout the United States and internationally as well. To contact her, call (800) 660-7395 or visit www.emic.org.

Suzanne Rentz is the founder and president of Daughters of Heaven Ministries and has been the keynote speaker for the Daughters of Heaven conferences as well as other conferences and women's meetings around the country. Suzanne's true passion is that young women discover God's love and acceptance, receive a revelation that they are created in His image, and uncover His plan for their lives. Suzanne, her husband, Mark, and their three children reside in Sacramento, California, where Mark is an associate pastor at River City Community Church. To contact Suzanne, call (866) 381-3882 or visit www.daughtersofheaven.org.

Carla Stephens serves in the youth ministry at World Changers Church International in College Park, Georgia, in addition to ministering in conferences, conventions, and workshops. She has served as the supervisor of Handmaidens of the Lord, an organization which trains and nurtures young women in their walk with God, and on the Women's Advisory Board alongside Pastor Taffi Dollar. Carla is a graduate of World Changers Church International School of Ministry and holds an associates degree in art from the Art Institute of Atlanta. Carla and her husband, Jesse, reside in the Atlanta, Georgia area with their sons, Evan and Ryan. To contact Carla, write Carla Stephens, P.O. Box 1630, Fayetteville, Georgia 30214 or email her at jcarstephens@msn.com.

Betsy Williams is a freelance editor/writer, specializing in inspirational books. Her work has appeared in publications from a variety of publishers in the Christian bookselling industry, including several major publishers. Originally from Huntsville, Alabama, she is a 1983 graduate of Rhema Bible Training Center in Tulsa, Oklahoma, where she and her family currently reside. Betsy and her husband, Jim, are the proud parents of two active boys. She may be contacted at williams.services.inc@cox.net.

Endnotes

[1] Lindsay Roberts, *Make Your Day Count* magazine (Tulsa, OK: Oral Roberts Evangelistic Association, Oct.–Dec. 2002) pp. 6–7.

[2] Terri Copeland Pearsons, "An Ambassador of Love" (Ft. Worth, TX: Kenneth Copeland Ministries) <http://www.kcm.org/studycenter/*articles*/relationships/ambassador_love.html> (accessed Sept. 2003).

[3] Eastman Curtis, *Xtreme Talk,* (Tulsa, OK: Harrison House Publishers, 2002) pp. 29,67.

[4] Eastman Curtis, *Make Your Day Count* magazine (July–Sept. 2003) p. 16.

[6] Dr. Patricia D. Bailey, *Finishing Touches,* (Tulsa, OK: Harrison House Publishers, 2003) pp. 196–204.

[7] Nancy Alcorn, *Mercy for Eating Disorders* (Tulsa, OK: Harrison House Publishers, 2003) pp. 11–15.

[8] Lindsay Roberts, *Make Your Day Count* magazine (Jan.–March 2003) pp. 7–8.

[9] Dee Simmons, *Make Your Day Count* magazine (Oct.–Dec. 2002) p. 25.

[10] Carla Stephens, *A Passion for Purity,* (Tulsa, OK: Harrison House Publishers, 2003) pp. 6–8.

[11] Kenneth and Gloria Copeland, *Load Up,* (Tulsa, OK: Harrison House Publishers, 2002) p. 19.

[12] Eastman Curtis, *Xtreme Talk,* p. 128.

[13] Dee Simmons, *Make Your Day Count* magazine (Oct.–Dec. 2002) p. 25.

[14] Phoenix Police Department, "Baby-sitting Tips," <http://www.ci.phoenix.az.us/POLICE/babysi1.html> (accessed Dec. 2003).

[15] Terri Copeland Pearsons, "An Ambassador of Love" (Ft. Worth, TX: Kenneth Copeland Ministries) <http://www.kcm.org/studycenter/articles/relationships/ambassador_love.html> (accessed Sept. 2003).

[16] Blaine Bartel, *Every Teenager's Little Black Book of Hard-To-Find Information,* p. 2.

[17] Lindsay Roberts, *Make Your Day Count* magazine (July–Sept. 2002) pp. 6–7.

[18] Nancy Alcorn, *Mercy for Eating Disorders,* pp. 43–47.

[19] Kate McVeigh, *The Blessing of Favor* (Tulsa, OK: Harrison House Publishers, 2003) pp. 3–12.

[20] Kenneth and Gloria Copeland, *Over the Edge Youth Devotional* (Tulsa, OK: Harrison House Publishers, 1998) p. 293.

[22] Blaine Bartel, *Every Teenager's Little Black Book of Hard-To-Find Information* (Tulsa, OK: Harrison House Publishers, 2002) p. 51.

[23] Eastman Curtis, *Xtreme Talk,* pp. 6,129.

[24] Kellie Copeland Kutz, "Make Sure Your Children Are Protected," <www.kcm.org> (accessed Sept. 2003); *Protecting Your Family in Dangerous Times* (Tulsa, OK: Harrison House Publishers 2002) pp. 4–8.

[25] Kate McVeigh, *Single and Loving It!* (Tulsa, OK: Harrison House Publishers, 2003) pp. 71–72.

[26] Lindsay Roberts, *Make Your Day Count* magazine (April–June 2001) pp. 9–12.

[27] Blaine Bartel, *Every Teenager's Little Black Book on Cool* (Tulsa, OK: Harrison House Publishers, 2002) pp. 6–7.

[28] Lindsay Roberts, *Richard & Lindsay Roberts Family Cookbook* (Tulsa, OK: Oral Roberts Evangelistic Association, 1990) p. 10.

[29] Kenneth and Gloria Copeland, *Load Up,* p. 105.

[30] Eastman Curtis, *Xtreme Talk,* pp. 12–13.

[31] The Nemours Foundation, "What You Need to Know About Drugs" <http://kidshealth.org/kid/grow/drugs_alcohol/know_drugs.html> (accessed Dec. 2003).

[32] *Keeping Your Kids Drug-Free* (National Youth Anti-Drug Media Campaign, Office of National Drug Control Policy) http://media.shs.net/prevline/pdfs/phd884.pdf> (accessed Dec. 2003) PDF, p. 14.

[33] Blaine Bartel, *Every Teenager's Little Black Book of Hard-To-Find Information,* pp. 27–28.

[34] Kenneth and Gloria Copeland, *Load Up,* p. 85.

[35] Kate McVeigh, *Single and Loving It!,* pp. 89–92.

[37] Sunny Golloway, Dallas Martin, Lonnie Murphy, Scott Campbell, *Make Your Day Count* magazine (July–Sept. 2003) p. 17.

[38] Suzanne Rentz, *Daughters of Heaven* (Tulsa, OK: Harrison House Publishers, 2003) pp. 152–153.

[39] Kenneth and Gloria Copeland, *Load Up,* p. 101.

[40] Eastman Curtis, *Xtreme Talk,* pp. 18,83.

[41] Blaine Bartel, *Every Teenager's Little Black Book of Hard-To-Find Information,* p. 1.

[42] Lindsay Roberts, *Make Your Day Count* magazine (April–June 2003) pp. 6–8.

[43] Blaine Bartel, *Oneighty® Devotional* (Tulsa, OK: Harrison House Publishers, 2003) pp. 84–85.

[44] Suzanne Rentz, *Daughters of Heaven,* pp. ix–x.

[45] Carla Stephens, *A Passion for Purity,* pp. 26–30.

[46] The Department of Health and Human Resources: Office of Maternal, Child and Family Health, Division of Infant, Child, and Adolescent Health, West Virginia Abstinence Education Project; <http://www.wvdhhr.org/mcfh/ICAH/Abstinence/refuse.htm> (accessed Dec. 2003).

[47] Kenneth and Gloria Copeland, *Load Up,* p. 38.

[48] Lindsay Roberts, *Make Your Day Count* magazine (Oct.–Dec. 2002) p. 6.

[49] Eastman Curtis, *Xtreme Talk,* pp. 18,20.

[50] The Department of Health and Human Resources: Office of Maternal, Child and Family Health, Division of Infant, Child, and Adolescent Health, West Virginia Abstinence Education Project; <http://www.wvdhhr.org/mcfh/ICAH/Abstinence/refuse.htm> (accessed Dec. 2003).

[51] Carla Stephens, *A Passion for Purity,* pp. 61–68.

[52] Kenneth and Gloria Copeland, *Load Up,* p. 35.

[53] Blaine Bartel, *Oneighty® Devotional,* p. 26.

[54] Suzanne Rentz, *Daughters of Heaven,* pp. xvii–xix.

[55] Blaine Bartel, *Every Teenager's Little Black Book of Hard-To-Find Information,* pp. 6–7.

[56] Kate McVeigh, *Single and Loving It!,* pp. 77–78.

[57] Lindsay Roberts, *Make Your Day Count* magazine (Tulsa, OK: Oral Roberts Evangelistic Association, Oct.–Dec. 2001) p. 8.

[58] Eastman Curtis, *Xtreme Talk,* p. 22.

[59] Blaine Bartel, *Every Teenager's Little Black Book of Hard-To-Find Information,* p. 47.

[60] *Make Your Day Count* magazine (Oct.–Dec. 2001) p. 17.

[61] Blaine Bartel, *Oneighty® Devotional,* pp. 121,123.

[62] Marty Copeland, *Miracles Now* (Tulsa, OK: Oral Roberts Evangelistic Association, July–Sept. 2003) p. 22.

[63] Kenneth and Gloria Copeland, *Load Up,* p. 124.

[64] Suzanne Rentz, *Daughters of Heavein,* pp. xix–xx.

[65] Lindsay Roberts, *Make Your Day Count* magazine (Oct.–Dec. 2001) p. 7.

[66] Eastman Curtis, *Xtreme Talk,* p. 45.

[67] Blaine Bartel, *Oneighty Devotional,* pp. 13-14.

[68] Blaine Bartel, *Little Black Book for Graduates* (Tulsa, OK: Harrison House Publishers) pp. 26–27.

[69] *Webster's New World College Dictionary,* 3d ed. (New York: Simon & Shuster, Inc., copyright 1997, 1996, 1994, 1991, 1988), s.v. "favor."

[70] Kate McVeigh, *The Blessing of Favor,* pp. 15–19.

[71] Kim Freeman, *Basic Training* (Tulsa, OK: Harrison House Publishers, 2003) pp. 15–17.

[72] Suzanne Rentz, *Daughters of Heaven,* p. xx.

[73] Kenneth and Gloria Copeland, *Load Up,* p. 46.
[75] Eastman Curtis, *Xtreme Talk,* pp. 14,159.
[76] Sarah Bowling, *Revival of the Bible* (Tulsa, OK: Harrison House Publishers, 2001) pp. 19–20.
[77] Blaine Bartel, *Every Teenager's Little Black Book of Hard-To-Find Information,* p. 8.
[78] Blaine Bartel, *Oneight® Devotional,* pp. 64,66.
[79] This is the author's paraphrased narrative of this part of Ezekiel 16 in which the Lord spoke to the prophet Ezekiel allegorically about Jerusalem.
[80] Suzanne Rentz, *Daughters of Heaven,* pp. xxi–xxii.
[81] James E. Strong, "Hebrew and Chaldee Dictionary" in *Strong's Exhaustive Concordance of the Bible* (Nashville, TN: Abingdon Press, 1890) p. 47, entry #3068, s.v. "Lord," Genesis 2:7.
[82] Sarah Bowling, *Revival of the Bible,* pp. 136–139.
[83] Kenneth and Gloria Copeland, *Load Up,* p. 259.
[84] Lindsay Roberts, *Miracles Now* (March–April 2000) p. 14.
[85] Eastman Curtis, *Xtreme Talk,* p. 28.
[86] Sarah Bowling, *Revival of the Bible,* pp. 27–28.
[87] Sarah Bowling, *Revival of the Bible,* pp. 28–29.
[88] Suzanne Rentz, *Daughters of Heaven,* p. ix.
[89] Blaine Bartel, *Oneighty® Devotional,* p. 29.
[90] Kenneth and Gloria Copeland, *Load Up,* p. 93.
[91] Psalm 139:14; Psalm 118:5; 2 Timothy 1:7; Jeremiah 31:3; and Ephesians 1:6.
[92] Nancy Alcorn, *Mercy for Eating Disorders,* pp. 110–111.
[93] Nancy Alcorn, *Mercy for Eating Disorders,* pp. 184–188.
[94] Lindsay Roberts, *Miracles Now* (Nov.–Dec. 2000) pp. 14–15.
[95] Eastman Curtis, *Xtreme Talk,* p. 39.
[96] Blaine Bartel, *Oneighty® Devotional,* p. 33.
[97] Sarah Bowling, *Revival of the Bible,* pp. 157–158.
[98] Kenneth and Gloria Copeland, *Load Up,* p. 113.
[99] Sarah Bowling, *Revival of the Bible,* p. 30.
[100] Eastman Curtis, *Xtreme Talk,* p. 9.
[101] Blaine Bartel, *Every Teenager's Little Black Book of Hard-To-Find Information,* p. 39.
[102] Nancy Alcorn, *Mercy for Eating Disorders,* pp. 114–115,118.
[103] Rentz, Suzanne, Daughters of Heaven, p. xii.
[104] Roberts, Lindsay, *36 Hours with an Angel* (Tulsa, OK: Oral Roberts Evangelistic Association, Inc., 1990) pp. 121–122,126.
[105] Blaine Bartel, *Every Teenager's Little Black Book of Hard-To-Find Information,* p. 18.
[106] Sarah Bowling, *Revival of the Bible,* pp. 30–32.
[107] Eastman Curtis, *Xtreme Talk,* pp. 35,68.
[108] Kenneth and Gloria Copeland, *Load Up,* p. 86.
[109] Blaine Bartel, *Oneighty® Devotional,* p. 31.
[110] Roberts, Lindsay, *StressLess Living* pp. 13–14.

Prayer of Salvation

God loves you—no matter who you are, no matter what your past. God loves you so much that He gave His one and only begotten Son for you. The Bible tells us that "whoever believes in him shall not perish but have eternal life" (John 3:16). Jesus laid down His life and rose again so that we could spend eternity with Him in heaven and experience His absolute best on earth. If you would like to receive Jesus into your life, say the following prayer out loud and mean it from your heart:

Heavenly Father, I come to You, admitting that I am a sinner. Right now, I choose to turn away from sin, and I ask You to cleanse me of all unrighteousness. I believe that Your Son, Jesus, died on the cross to take away my sins. I also believe that He rose again from the dead so that I might be forgiven of my sins and made righteous through faith in Him. I call upon the name of Jesus Christ to be the Savior and Lord of my life. Jesus, I choose to follow You and ask that You fill me with the power of the Holy Spirit. I declare that right now I am a child of God. I am free from sin and full of the righteousness of God. I am saved in Jesus' name. Amen.

If you prayed this prayer to receive Jesus Christ as your Lord and Savior for the first time, please contact us on the Web at **www.harrisonhouse.com** to receive a free book.

Or you may write to us at

Harrison House
P.O. Box 35035
Tulsa, Oklahoma 74153

Other Books in the Make Your Day Count Devotional Series

Make Your Day Count Devotional for Women
Make Your Day Count Devotional for Teachers
Make Your Day Count Devotional for Mothers

Additional copies of this book
are available from your local bookstore.

If this book has been a blessing to you
or if you would like to see more of the
Harrison House product line,
please visit us on our Web site at
www.harrisonhouse.com.

HARRISON HOUSE
Tulsa, Oklahoma 74153

The Harrison House Vision

Proclaiming the truth and the power
Of the Gospel of Jesus Christ
With excellence;

Challenging Christians to
Live victoriously,
Grow spiritually,
Know God intimately.